MW00634988

Principles
in Practice

The Principles in Practice imprint offers teachers concrete illustrations of effective classroom practices based in NCTE research briefs and policy statements. Each book discusses the research on a specific topic, links the research to an NCTE brief or policy statement, and then demonstrates how those principles come alive in practice: by showcasing actual classroom practices that demonstrate the policies in action; by talking about research in practical, teacher-friendly language; and by offering teachers possibilities for rethinking their own practices in light of the ideas presented in the books. Books within the imprint are grouped in strands, each strand focused on a significant topic of interest.

Volumes in the Adolescent Literacy Strand

Adolescent Literacy at Risk? The Impact of Standards (2009) Rebecca Bowers Sipe

Adolescents and Digital Literacies: Learning Alongside Our Students (2010) Sara Kajder

Adolescent Literacy and the Teaching of Reading: Lessons Learned from a Teacher of Literature (2010) Deborah Appleman

Volumes in the Writing in Today's Classrooms Strand

Writing in the Dialogical Classroom: Students and Teachers Responding to the Texts of Their Lives (2011) Bob Fecho

Writing in the Dialogical Classroom

Students and Teachers Responding to the Texts of Their Lives

Bob Fecho
University of Georgia

National Council of Teachers of English
1111 W. Kenyon Road, Urbana, Illinois 61801-1096

Staff Editors: Carol Roehm and Bonny Graham

Imprint Editor: Cathy Fleischer

Interior Design: Victoria Pohlmann

Cover Design: Pat Mayer

NCTE Stock Number: 13578

Library of Congress Cataloging-in-Publication Data

Fecho, Bob.
    Writing in the dialogical classroom : students and teachers responding to the texts of their lives / Bob Fecho.
        p. cm.
    Includes biliographical references and index.
    ISBN 978-0-8141-1357-8 ((pbk) : alk. paper)
    1. Composition (Language arts) 2. English language—Composition and exercises—Study and teaching. I. National Council of Teachers of English. II. Title.
    LB1576.F395 2011
    808'.042071—dc22
                                                                2010053451

To Marci Resnick, who taught me more about working with colleagues in our brief time together than I learned in all my years of higher education.

Contents

Acknowledgments

I have been blessed in my various writing projects to have excellent editors, ones who know how to both push and praise with skill and thought. Cathy Fleischer stands tall among them, and I thank her for her empathy, her cheerleading, her incisive questioning, her good humor, and her deep appreciation of Bruce. I also need to thank Carol Roehm for copyediting with a light touch and sensitivity for my word choices and cadences.

My partner and colleague, Janette Hill, whenever I write, is subject to endless queries and frequent myopic preoccupation on my part. She handles all with patience and intelligence, and my gratitude is but small recompense.

Dog Sage and cat dipi cope with benign inattention, late feedings, and rhetorical questions they choose not to answer. I thank them for their forbearance.

The twelve teachers profiled in this book—Ian Altman, Kristi Amatucci, Paige Cole, Soria Colomer, Dawan Coombs, Angela Dean, Lisa Hall, Emily Pendergrass, Sarah Skinner, Trevor Stewart, Russ Turpin, and Amy Alexandra Wilson—contributed precious time, perceptive feedback, unquestioned expertise, and positive thoughts. The book could not have been written without their input and the teaching practices they so lovingly constructed. My debt to them is huge.

NCTE Beliefs about the Teaching of Writing

Just as the nature of and expectation for literacy has changed in the past century and a half, so has the nature of writing. Much of that change has been due to technological developments, from pen and paper, to typewriter, to word processor, to networked computer, to design software capable of composing words, images, and sounds. These developments not only expanded the types of texts that writers produce, they also expanded immediate access to a wider variety of readers. With full recognition that writing is an increasingly multifaceted activity, we offer several principles that should guide effective teaching practice.

Everyone has the capacity to write, writing can be taught, and teachers can help students become better writers

Though poets and novelists may enjoy debating whether or not writing can be taught, teachers of writing have more pragmatic aims. Setting aside the question of whether one can learn to be an artistic genius, there is ample empirical evidence that anyone can get better at writing, and that what teachers do makes a difference in how much students are capable of achieving as writers.

Developing writers require support. This support can best come through carefully designed writing instruction oriented toward acquiring new strategies and skills. Certainly, writers can benefit from teachers who simply support and give them time to write. However, instruction matters. Teachers of writing should be well-versed in composition theory and research, and they should know methods for turning that theory into practice. When writing teachers first walk into classrooms, they should already know and practice good composition. However, much as in doctoring, learning to teach well is a lifetime process, and lifetime professional development is the key to successful practice. Students deserve no less.

People learn to write by writing

As is the case with many other things people do, getting better at writing requires doing it—a lot. This means actual writing, not merely listening to lectures about writing, doing grammar drills, or discussing readings. The more people write, the easier it gets and the more they are motivated to do it. Writers who write a lot learn more about the process because they have had more experience inside it. Writers learn from each session with their hands on a keyboard or around a pencil as they draft, rethink, revise, and draft again. Thinking about how to make your writing better is what revision is. In other words, improvement is built into the experience of writing.

What does this mean for teaching?

Writing instruction must include ample in-class and out-of-class opportunities for writing and should include writing for a variety of purposes and audiences.

Writing, though, should not be viewed as an activity that happens only within a classroom's walls. Teachers need to support students in the development of writing lives, habits,

NCTE Beliefs about the Teaching of Writing

and preferences for life outside school. We already know that many students do extensive amounts of self-sponsored writing: emailing, keeping journals or doing creative projects, instant messaging, making Web sites, blogging, and so on. As much as possible, instruction should be geared toward making sense in a life outside of school, so that writing has ample room to grow in individuals' lives. It is useful for teachers to consider what elements of their curriculum they could imagine students self-sponsoring outside of school. Ultimately, those are the activities that will produce more writing.

In order to provide quality opportunities for student writing, teachers must minimally understand:

- How to interpret curriculum documents, including things that can be taught while students are actually writing, rather than one thing at a time to all students at once.
- The elements of "writing lives" as people construct them in the world outside of school.
- Social structures that support independent work.
- How to confer with individual writers.
- How to assess while students are writing.
- How to plan what students need to know in response to ongoing research.
- How to create a sense of personal safety in the classroom, so that students are willing to write freely and at length.
- How to create community while students are writing in the same room together.

Writing is a process

Often, when people think of writing, they think of texts—finished pieces of writing. Understanding what writers do, however, involves thinking not just about what texts look like when they are finished but also about what strategies writers might employ to produce those texts. Knowledge about writing is only complete with understanding the complex of actions in which writers engage as they produce texts. Such understanding has two aspects. First is the development, through extended practice over years, of a repertory of routines, skills, strategies, and practices for generating, revising, and editing different kinds of texts. Second is the development of reflective abilities and meta-awareness about writing. This procedural understanding helps writers most when they encounter difficulty, or when they are in the middle of creating a piece of writing. How does someone get started? What do they do when they get stuck? How do they plan the overall process, each section of their work, and even the rest of the sentence they are writing right now? Research, theory, and practice over the past 40 years has produced a richer understanding of what writers do—those who are proficient and professional as well as those who struggle.

Two further points are vital. To say that writing is a process is decidedly not to say that it should—or can—be turned into a formulaic set of steps. Experienced writers shift between different operations according to tasks and circumstances. Second, writers do not accumulate process skills and strategies once and for all. They develop and refine writing skills throughout their writing lives.

NCTE Beliefs about the Teaching of Writing

What does this mean for teaching?

Whenever possible, teachers should attend to the process that students might follow to produce texts—and not only specify criteria for evaluating finished products, in form or content. Students should become comfortable with prewriting techniques, multiple strategies for developing and organizing a message, a variety of strategies for revising and editing, and strategies for preparing products for public audiences and for deadlines. In explaining assignments, teachers should provide guidance and options for ways of going about it. Sometimes, evaluating the processes students follow—the decisions they make, the attempts along the way—can be as important as evaluating the final product. At least some of the time, the teacher should guide the students through the process, assisting them as they go. Writing instruction must provide opportunities for students to identify the processes that work best for themselves as they move from one writing situation to another.

Writing instruction must also take into account that a good deal of workplace writing and other writing takes place in collaborative situations. Writers must learn to work effectively with one another.

Teachers need to understand at least the following in order to be excellent at teaching writing as a process:

- The relationship between features of finished writing and the actions writers perform.
- What writers of different genres say about their craft.
- The process of writing from the inside, that is, what they themselves as writers experience in a host of different writing situations.
- Multiple strategies for approaching a wide range of typical problems writers face during composing, including strategies for audience and task analysis, invention, revision, and editing.
- Multiple models of the writing process, the varied ways individuals approach similar tasks, and the ways that writing situations and genres inform processes.
- Published texts, immediately available, that demonstrate a wide range of writing strategies and elements of craft.
- The relationships among the writing process, curriculum, learning, and pedagogy.
- How to design time for students to do their best work on an assignment.
- How writers use tools, including word-processing and design software and computer-based resources.

Writing is a tool for thinking

When writers actually write, they think of things that they did not have in mind before they began writing. The act of writing generates ideas. This is different from the way we often think of writers—as getting ideas fixed in their heads before they write them down. The notion that writing is a medium for thought is important in several ways. It suggests a number of important uses for writing: to solve problems, to identify issues, to construct questions, to

NCTE Beliefs about the Teaching of Writing

Writing as a tool for thinking

reconsider something one had already figured out, to try out a half-baked idea. This insight that writing is a tool for thinking helps us to understand the process of drafting and revision as one of exploration and discovery, and is nothing like transcribing from prerecorded tape. The writing process is not one of simply fixing up the mistakes in an early draft, but of finding more and more wrinkles and implications in what one is talking about.

What does this mean for teaching?

In any writing classroom, some of the writing is for others and some of the writing is for the writer. Regardless of the age, ability, or experience of the writer, the use of writing to generate thought is still valuable; therefore, forms of writing such as personal narrative, journals, written reflections, observations, and writing-to-learn strategies are important.

In any writing assignment, it must be assumed that part of the work of writers will involve generating and regenerating ideas prior to writing them.

Excellence in teaching writing as thinking requires that the teacher understand:

- Varied tools for thinking through writing, such as journals, writers' notebooks, blogs, sketchbooks, digital portfolios, listservs or online discussion groups, dialogue journals, double-entry or dialectical journals, and others.
- The kinds of new thinking that occur when writers revise.
- The variety of types of thinking people do when they compose, and what those types of thinking look like when they appear in writing.
- Strategies for getting started with an idea, or finding an idea when one does not occur immediately.

Writing grows out of many different purposes

Purposes for writing include developing social networks; engaging in civic discourse; supporting personal and spiritual growth; reflecting on experience; communicating professionally and academically; building relationships with others, including friends, family, and like-minded individuals; and engaging in aesthetic experiences.

Writing is not just one thing. It varies in form, structure, and production process according to its audience and purpose. A note to a cousin is not like a business report, which is different again from a poem. The processes and ways of thinking that lead up to these varied kinds of texts can also vary widely, from the quick single-draft email to a friend to the careful drafting and redrafting of a legal contract. The different purposes and forms both grow out of and create various relationships between the writer and the potential reader, and relationships reflected in degrees of formality in language, as well as assumptions about what knowledge and experience is already shared, and what needs to be explained. Writing with certain purposes in mind, the writer focuses her attention on what the audience is thinking or believing; other times, the writer focuses more on the information she is organizing, or on her own thoughts and feelings. Therefore, the thinking, the procedures, and the physical format in writing all differ when writers' purposes vary.

NCTE Beliefs about the Teaching of Writing

What does this mean for teaching?

Often, in school, students write only to prove that they did something they were asked to do, in order to get credit for it. Or, students are taught a single type of writing and are led to believe this type will suffice in all situations. Writers outside of school have many different purposes beyond demonstrating accountability, and they practice myriad types and genres. In order to make sure students are learning how writing differs when the purpose and the audience differ, it is important that teachers create opportunities for students to be in different kinds of writing situations, where the relationships and agendas are varied. Even within academic settings, the characteristics of good writing vary among disciplines; what counts as a successful lab report, for example, differs from a successful history paper, essay exam, or literary interpretation.

In order to teach for excellence about purposes in writing, teachers need to understand:

- The wide range of purposes for which people write, and the forms of writing that arise from those purposes.
- Strategies and forms for writing for public participation in a democratic society.⎤✶
- Ways people use writing for personal growth, expression, and reflection, and how to encourage and develop this kind of writing.
- Aesthetic or artistic forms of writing and how they are made. That is, the production of creative and literary texts, for the purposes of entertainment, pleasure, or exploration.
- Appropriate forms for varied academic disciplines and the purposes and relationships that create those forms.
- Ways of organizing and transforming school curricula in order to provide students with adequate education in varied purposes for writing.
- How to set up a course to write for varied purposes and audiences.

Conventions of finished and edited texts are important to readers and therefore to writers

Readers expect writing to conform to their expectations, to match the conventions generally established for public texts. Contemporary readers expect words to be spelled in a standardized way, for punctuation to be used in predictable ways, for usage and syntax to match that used in texts they already acknowledge as successful. They expect the style in a piece of writing to be appropriate to its genre and social situation. In other words, it is important that writing that goes public be "correct."

What does this mean for teaching?

Every teacher has to resolve a tension between writing as generating and shaping ideas and writing as demonstrating expected surface conventions. On the one hand, it is important for writing to be as correct as possible and for students to be able to produce correct texts. On the other hand, achieving correctness is only one set of things writers must be able to do; a correct text empty of ideas or unsuited to its audience or purpose is not a good piece

NCTE Beliefs about the Teaching of Writing

of writing. There is no formula for resolving this tension. Writing is both/and: both fluency and fitting conventions. Research shows that facility in these two operations often develops unevenly. For example, as students learn increasingly sophisticated ways of thinking (for example, conditional or subordinate reasoning) or dealing with unfamiliar content, they may produce more surface errors, or perhaps even seem to regress. This is because their mental energies are focused on the new intellectual challenges. Such uneven development is to be tolerated, in fact, encouraged. It is rather like strength gains from lifting weight, which actually tears down muscle fibers only to stimulate them to grow back stronger. Too much emphasis on correctness can actually inhibit development. By the same token, without mastering conventions for written discourse, writers' efforts may come to naught. Drawing readers' attention to the gap between the text at hand and the qualities of texts they expect causes readers to not attend to the content. Each teacher must be knowledgeable enough about the entire landscape of writing instruction to guide particular students toward a goal, developing both increasing fluency in new contexts and mastery of conventions. NCTE's stated policy over many years has been that conventions of writing are best taught in the context of writing. Simply completing workbook or online exercises is inadequate if students are not regularly producing meaningful texts themselves.

Most writing teachers teach students how to edit their writing that will go out to audiences. This is often considered a late stage in the process of composing, because editing is only essential for the words that are left after all the cutting, replacing, rewriting, and adding that go on during revision. Writers need an image in their minds of conventional grammar, spelling, and punctuation in order to compare what is already on the page to an ideal of correctness. They also need to be aware of stylistic options that will produce the most desirable impression on their readers. All of the dimensions of editing are motivated by a concern for an audience.

Teachers should be familiar with techniques for teaching editing and encouraging reflective knowledge about editing conventions. For example, some find it useful to have students review a collection of their writing over time—a journal, notebook, folder, or portfolio—to study empirically the way their writing has changed or needs to change, with respect to conventions. A teacher might say, "Let's look at all the times you used commas," or "Investigate the ways you might have combined sentences." Such reflective appointments permit students to set goals for their own improvement.

Teachers need to understand at least the following in order to be excellent at teaching conventions to writers:

- Research on developmental factors in writing ability, including the tension between fluency with new operations or contents and the practice of accepted spelling, punctuation, syntactic, and usage conventions.
- The diverse influences and constraints on writers' decision making as they determine the kinds of conventions that apply to this situation and this piece of writing.
- A variety of applications and options for most conventions.
- The appropriate conventions for academic classroom English.
- How to teach usage without excessive linguistic terminology.

NCTE Beliefs about the Teaching of Writing

- The linguistic terminology that is necessary for teaching particular kinds of usage.
- The linguistic terminology necessary for communicating professionally with other educators.
- The relationship among rhetorical considerations and decisions about conventions, for example, the conditions under which a dash, a comma, a semicolon, or a full stop might be more effective.
- Conventions beyond the sentence, such as effective uses of bulleted lists, mixed genres and voices, diagrams and charts, design of pages, and composition of video shots.
- An understanding of the relationship among conventions in primary and secondary discourses.
- The conditions under which people learn to do new things with language.
- The relationship between fluency, clarity, and correctness in writing development and the ability to assess which is the leading edge of the student's learning now.

Writing and reading are related

Writing and reading are related. People who read a lot have a much easier time getting better at writing. In order to write a particular kind of text, it helps if the writer has read that kind of text. In order to take on a particular style of language, the writer needs to have read that language, to have heard it in her mind, so that she can hear it again in order to compose it.

Writing can also help people become better readers. In their earliest writing experiences, children listen for the relationships of sounds to letters, which contributes greatly to their phonemic awareness and phonics knowledge. Writers also must learn how texts are structured, because they have to create them. The experience of plotting a short story, organizing a research report, or making line breaks in a poem permits the writer, as a reader, to approach new reading experiences with more informed eyes.

Additionally, reading is a vital source of information and ideas. For writers fully to contribute to a given topic or to be effective in a given situation, they must be familiar with what previous writers have said. Reading also creates a sense of what one's audience knows or expects on a topic.

What does this mean for teaching?

One way to help students become better writers is to make sure they have lots of extended time to read, in school and out. Most research indicates that the easiest way to tap motivation to read is to teach students to choose books and other texts they understand and enjoy, and then to give them time in school to read them. In addition to making students stronger readers, this practice makes them stronger writers.

Students should also have access to and experience in reading material that presents both published and student writing in various genres. Through immersion in a genre, students develop an internalized sense of why an author would select a particular genre for a particular purpose, the power of a particular genre to convey a message, and the rhetorical constraints and possibilities inherent in a genre. Students should be taught the features of different genres, experientially not only explicitly, so that they develop facilities in producing them and become familiar with variant features. If one is going to write in a genre, it is very helpful to have read in that genre first.

Overall, frequent conversations about the connections between what we read and what we write are helpful. These connections will sometimes be about the structure and craft of the writing itself, and sometimes about thematic and content connections.

In order to do an excellent job of teaching into the connections of writing and reading, teachers need to understand at least these things:

- How writers read in a special way, with an eye toward not just what the text says but how it is put together.
- The psychological and social processes reading and writing have in common.
- The ways writers form and use constructs of their intended readers, anticipating their responses and needs.
- An understanding of text structure that is fluid enough to accommodate frequent disruptions.

Writing has a complex relationship to talk

From its beginnings in early childhood through the most complex setting imaginable, writing exists in a nest of talk. Conversely, speakers usually write notes and, regularly, scripts, and they often prepare visual materials that include texts and images. Writers often talk in order to rehearse the language and content that will go into what they write, and conversation often provides an impetus or occasion for writing. They sometimes confer with teachers and other writers about what to do next, how to improve their drafts, or in order to clarify their ideas and purposes. Their usual ways of speaking sometimes do and sometimes do not feed into the sentences they write, depending on an intricate set of decisions writers make continually. One of the features of writing that is most evident and yet most difficult to discuss is the degree to which it has "voice." The fact that we use this term, even in the absence of actual sound waves, reveals some of the special relationship between speech and writing.

What does this mean for teaching?

In early writing, we can expect lots of talk to surround writing, since what children are doing is figuring out how to get speech onto paper. Early teaching in composition should also attend to helping children get used to producing language orally, through telling stories, explaining how things work, predicting what will happen, and guessing about why things and people are the way they are. Early writing experiences will include students explaining orally what is in a text, whether it is printed or drawn.

As they grow, writers still need opportunities to talk about what they are writing about, to rehearse the language of their upcoming texts, and to run ideas by trusted colleagues before taking the risk of committing words to paper. After making a draft, it is often helpful for writers to discuss with peers what they have done, partly in order to get ideas from their peers, partly to see what they, the writers, say when they try to explain their thinking. Writing conferences, wherein student writers talk about their work with a teacher, who can make suggestions or re-orient what the writer is doing, are also very helpful uses of talk in the writing process.

To take advantage of the strong relationships between talk and writing, teachers must minimally understand:

- Ways of setting up and managing student talk in partnerships and groups.
- Ways of establishing a balance between talk and writing in classroom management.
- Ways of organizing the classroom and/or schedule to permit individual teacher-student conferences.
- Strategies for deliberate insertions of opportunities for talk into the writing process: knowing when and how students should talk about their writing.
- Ways of anticipating and solving interpersonal conflicts that arise when students discuss writing.
- Group dynamics in classrooms.
- Relationships—both similarities and differences—between oral and literate language.
- The uses of writing in public presentations and the values of students making oral presentations that grow out of and use their writing.

Literate practices are embedded in complicated social relationships

Writing happens in the midst of a web of relationships. There is, most obviously, the relationship between the writer and the reader. That relationship is often very specific: writers have a definite idea of who will read their words, not just a generalized notion that their text will be available to the world. Furthermore, particular people surround the writer—other writers, partners in purposes, friends, members of a given community—during the process of composing. They may know what the writer is doing and be indirectly involved in it, though they are not the audience for the work. In workplace and academic settings, writers write because someone in authority tells them to. Therefore, power relationships are built into the writing situation. In every writing situation, the writer, the reader, and all relevant others live in a structured social order, where some people's words count more than others, where being heard is more difficult for some people than others, where some people's words come true and others' do not.

Writers start in different places. It makes a difference what kind of language a writer spoke while growing up, and what kinds of language they are being asked to take on later in their experience. It makes a difference, too, the culture a writer comes from, the ways people use language in that culture, and the degree to which that culture is privileged in the larger society. Important cultural differences are not only ethnic but also racial, economic, geographical, and ideological. For example, rural students from small communities will have different language experiences than suburban students from comprehensive high schools, and students who come from very conservative backgrounds in which certain texts

NCTE Beliefs about the Teaching of Writing

are privileged or excluded will have different language experiences than those from progressive backgrounds in which the same is true. How much a writer has access to wide, diverse experiences and means of communication creates predispositions and skill for composing for an audience.

What does this mean for teaching?

The teaching of writing should assume students will begin with the sort of language with which they are most at home and most fluent in their speech. That language may be a dialect of English, or even a different language altogether. The goal is not to leave students where they are, however, but to move them toward greater flexibility, so that they can write not just for their own intimates but for wider audiences. Even as they move toward more widely used English, it is not necessary or desirable to wipe out the ways their family and neighborhood of origin use words. The teaching of excellence in writing means adding language to what already exists, not subtracting. The goal is to make more relationships available, not fewer.

In order to teach for excellence, a writing teacher needs understandings like these about contexts of language:

- How to find out about a students' language use in the home and neighborhoods, the changes in language context they may have encountered in their lives, and the kinds of language they most value.
- That wider social situations in which students write, speak, read, and relate to other people affect what seems "natural" or "easy" to them—or not. How to discuss with students the need for flexibility in the employment of different kinds of language for different social contexts.
- How to help students negotiate maintenance of their most familiar language while mastering academic classroom English and the varieties of English used globally.
- Control and awareness of their own varied languages and linguistic contexts.
- An understanding of the relationships among group affiliation, identity, and language.
- Knowledge of the usual patterns of common dialects in English, such as African American English, Spanish and varieties of English related to Spanish, common patterns in American rural and urban populations, predictable patterns in the English varieties of groups common in their teaching contexts.
- How and why to study a community's ways of using language.

Composing occurs in different modalities and technologies

Increasingly rapid changes in technologies mean that composing is involving a combination of modalities, such as print, still images, video, and sound. Computers make it possible for these modalities to combine in the same work environment. Connections to the Internet not only make a range of materials available to writers, they also collapse distances between writers and readers and between generating words and creating designs. Print always has a visual component, even if it is only the arrangement of text on a page and the type font.

NCTE Beliefs about the Teaching of Writing

Furthermore, throughout history, print has often been partnered with pictures in order to convey more meaning, to add attractiveness, and to appeal to a wider audience. Television, video, and film all involve such combinations, as do websites and presentation software. As basic tools for communicating expand to include modes beyond print alone, "writing" comes to mean more than scratching words with pen and paper. Writers need to be able to think about the physical design of text, about the appropriateness and thematic content of visual images, about the integration of sound with a reading experience, and about the medium that is most appropriate for a particular message, purpose, and audience.

What does this mean for teaching?

Writing instruction must accommodate the explosion in technology from the world around us.

From the use of basic word processing to support drafting, revision, and editing to the use of hypertext and the infusion of visual components in writing, the definition of what writing instruction includes must evolve to embrace new requirements.

Many teachers and students do not, however, have adequate access to computing, recording, and video equipment to take advantage of the most up-to-date technologies. In many cases, teaching about the multimodal nature of writing is best accomplished through varying the forms of writing with more ordinary implements. Writing picture books allows students to think between text and images, considering the ways they work together and distribute the reader's attention. Similar kinds of visual/verbal thinking can be supported through other illustrated text forms, including some kinds of journals/sketchbooks and posters. In addition, writing for performance requires the writer to imagine what the audience will see and hear and thus draws upon multiple modes of thinking, even in the production of a print text. Such uses of technology without the latest equipment reveal the extent to which "new" literacies are rooted also in older ones.

Teachers need to understand at least the following in order to be excellent at teaching composition as involving multiple media:

- A range of new genres that have emerged with the increase in electronic communication. Because these genres are continually evolving, this knowledge must be continually updated.
- Operation of some of the hardware and software their students will use, including resources for solving software and hardware problems.
- Internet resources for remaining up to date on technologies.
- Design principles for webpages.
- Email and chat conventions.
- How to navigate both the World Wide Web and Web-based databases.
- The use of software for making websites, including basic html, such as how to make a link.
- Theory about the relationship between print and other modalities.

NCTE Beliefs about the Teaching of Writing

Assessment of writing involves complex, informed, human judgment

Assessment of writing occurs for different purposes. Sometimes, a teacher assesses in order to decide what the student has achieved and what he or she still needs to learn. Sometimes, an entity beyond the classroom assesses a student's level of achievement in order to say whether they can go on to some new educational level that requires the writer to be able to do certain things. At other times, school authorities require a writing test in order to pressure teachers to teach writing. Still other times, as in a history exam, the assessment of writing itself is not the point, but the quality of the writing is evaluated almost in passing. In any of these assessments of writing, complex judgments are formed. Such judgments should be made by human beings, not machines. Furthermore, they should be made by professionals who are informed about writing, development, and the field of literacy education.

What does this mean for teaching?

Instructors of composition should know about various methods of assessment of student writing. Instructors must recognize the difference between formative and summative evaluation and be prepared to evaluate students' writing from both perspectives. By formative evaluation here, we mean provisional, ongoing, in-process judgments about what students know and what to teach next. By summative evaluation, we mean final judgments about the quality of student work. Teachers of writing must also be able to recognize the developmental aspects of writing ability and devise appropriate lessons for students at all levels of expertise.

Teachers need to understand at least the following in order to be excellent at writing assessment:

- How to find out what student writers can do, informally, on an ongoing basis.
- How to use that assessment in order to decide what and how to teach next.
- How to assess occasionally, less frequently than above, in order to form judgments about the quality of student writing and learning.
- How to assess ability and knowledge across multiple different writing engagements.
- What the features of good writing are, appropriate to the context and purposes of the teaching and learning.
- What the elements of a constructive process of writing are, appropriate to the context and purposes of the teaching and learning.

NCTE Beliefs about the Teaching of Writing

- What growth in writing looks like, the developmental aspects of writing ability.
- Ways of assessing student metacognitive process of the reading/writing connection.
- How to recognize in student writing (both in their texts and in their actions) the nascent potential for excellence at the features and processes desired.
- How to deliver useful feedback, appropriate for the writer and the situation.
- How to analyze writing situations for their most essential elements, so that assessment is not of everything about writing all at once, but rather is targeted to objectives.
- How to analyze and interpret both qualitative and quantitative writing assessments.
- How to evaluate electronic texts.
- How to use portfolios to assist writers in their development.
- How self-assessment and reflection contribute to a writer's development and ability to move among genres, media, and rhetorical situations.

A guideline by the Writing Study Group of the NCTE Executive Committee, November 2004

Sketching the Dialogical Classroom

Ashley, a college junior, wrote the following excerpt while she was a student in an undergraduate content area literacy course I taught a few years back at the University of Georgia. I had asked her and her classmates to write an essay about what each, as a preservice teacher, had come to understand about the importance of using reading and writing to better teach content. What follows is her introductory paragraph to a longer essay.

> Content literacy in all content areas, such as language arts, social studies, mathematics, and science entails that students obtain and direct writing and reading tactics to gain knowledge. Although literacy is expected from students in all content areas, it is necessary to convey that this is not factual information. However, it is an educator's duty to assist their students in reading and writing comprehension in each content area. Lacking content literacy skills in any subject will inhibit a student's ability to create significance and achieve understanding. Incorporating reading and writing instruction is a job for all teachers no matter the grade or subject area. Therefore, the content area I have selected to direct my focus is Social Studies, which is my second area of specialization. Reading and writing tribulations can hinder a student's improvement and generate unnecessary obstacles to perceiving the social studies subject matter. With that said, there are numerous issues that frighten me and, simultaneously, fascinate me about content literacy in social studies.

Before you read on, I suggest you think about what you would do if you were to sit down with Ashley for a writing conference? How would you counsel her? What questions would you ask? How would you talk about the strengths of this paper while also helping her consider what might be less successful?

Go ahead. Think about it. I'll wait.

On first glance, Ashley comes across as a young woman with a sound grasp of the English language and many of its conventions. Words are spelled correctly, punctuation is in place, word usage is crisp, and the text has the semblance, if not timbre, of academic writing. I know of many high school teachers who, having worked with students struggling with writing mechanics, would fall to their knees to have a student produce this paragraph.

But those same teachers, upon a more considered look at Ashley's introduction, would most likely want to raise some questions. For all of its correctness, the paragraph barely speaks to anyone, least of all Ashley. She has not created what Lysaker (2006) has called a relationship to text; therefore, she has removed herself from the writing by approximating the language of the academy and falling back on paragraph-writing formulas that held her in good stead through her high school education. The writing feels close-ended and deterministic. There is little sense that what she is committing to paper is going anywhere of depth or interest, or that new thoughts might be uncovered in the process. Instead, she has written an intro-duction—indeed, an entire essay as it turned out—in which the only context was the assignment I gave and the only purpose of being seemed to be that assignment.

My intent here is not to demean Ashley or the many writers who, like her, are products of their education. When she wrote this introduction, I'm sure she was, yet again, calling upon her experience writing countless five-paragraph essays based on decontextualized prompts, putting forth what she thought I wanted. But isn't that part of the issue? Ashley tends to see writing in school as something that, in the end, belongs to teachers. You write to please them as opposed to writing to make meaning for yourself and others. Outside the writing classroom, Ashley might be a writer of fluid and vivid prose, but in school she resorts to a style that was practiced repeatedly and most likely brought her praise for those efforts.

Although I had taken care, both in written instructions and through discus-sion, to point out the importance of bringing a sense of self even to academic writing, Ashley felt, most likely based on past experience, that she had good reason to doubt me. I wouldn't be surprised if she had been taught by at least one English teacher who had insisted that the way Ashley wrote in the introduction was what "they expect you to do in college." In fact, her work is exemplary of the writing I too often see produced in the kinds of high school and college composition class-rooms where writing is taught through recipes and formulas: mechanically correct, but largely lacking a sense of purpose or identity.

[handwritten margin note: relationship to text]

[handwritten margin note: ※ mechanically correct, but largely lacking a sense or purpose or identity]

Ashley's excerpt doesn't feel natural. Stolidity has to be carefully taught. I suspect that she didn't enter high school writing in ways that completely separate who she is and what she cares about from how she represents herself in text. I doubt that a sentence such as "Reading and writing tribulations can hinder a student's improvement and generate unnecessary obstacles to perceiving the social studies subject matter" flowed easily and organically for Ashley. Such writing is imposed on young writers. It is the teaching equivalent of dressing children in formal attire so they look good for the family photograph, even though the tight collars, stiff hairstyles, and rigid poses have nothing to do with who that child is 99 percent of the time.

need to tap into our innate abilities for language and communication

Having taught English for more than twenty years in an urban school district, I deeply understand how teachers feel conflicted when their time is constrained by overly invasive curricula and the pressure for narrowly defined success is applied by high-stakes testing. When confronted with imposed instructional "choices," a perceived inclination toward expediency on the part of their students, unreasonable expectations by administration to have students perform well on decontextualized tests, and an impossibly short time within which to manage all this effort, teachers tend to stress what they view as the practical option. That option, too often, turns out to be persuasive essays packaged in the five-paragraph format, a genre of writing they and their supervisors argue will help students in professional and academic venues, even if they have concerns as to how well such instruction works.

Despite these impediments, Ashley has much going for her. She's White and middle class, and that accident of birth grants her many privileges not afforded others. She started her education with her language and culture closely aligned with that of the school. She, on a daily basis, saw others like her in positions of authority and responsibility. When she opened books to read, from the very first basal reader to her senior year literature course, Ashley recognized the people, events, and contexts of her life there on the pages. And even though the school might have wanted her to dress her prose in old-fashioned collar stays and cuff links, the mainstream culture had so embraced her that the trade-off of self for a distanced formality seemed a small sacrifice. She was confident of who she was and what she could do because what she saw in media and experienced in life had confirmed her potential.

But not all students come to school perched in the comforting embrace of mainstream culture. The Latina living in rural Georgia whose parents have immigrated legally nevertheless spends the day fretting that one day she'll come home from school to find that immigration officers have swept her parents into custody. The child in the double-wide whose father runs a crystal meth operation worries about every police siren he hears. The rising senior on the wrestling team spends his Saturday mornings at the mall bookstore furtively reading gay magazines for insight into who he is and how to best reveal himself to others. The African American young woman, who often misses school to watch her younger siblings because Mom and Dad work late hours, writes and signs her own absence excuses. The recent Korean immigrant spends long days doing nothing of substance at the mall rather than face the long days of doing nothing of substance in school. How are their cultures celebrated in classrooms? When do their issues get addressed? What in their writing opportunities helps them to devise their sense of self and become better writers at the same time?

That's what this book is about: creating ample opportunities for students to use writing to explore who they are becoming and how they relate to the larger culture around them. I attempt to carve out space in literacy classrooms for an approach to writing that is more dialogical. Focused on adolescent learners, this approach seeks to develop writing experiences in schools that are reflective across time. Such writing should not be at the sacrifice of learning content and craft, but, instead, will foster even deeper explorations of such. To reflect on the experiences of William Shakespeare's Juliet, Sandra Cisneros's Esperanza, or Sister Souljah's Winter is to reflect on self. In this text, I create an ongoing conversation between classroom practice, theory, and research to show how each informs the others. Ultimately, my intent is to illustrate the need for empowerment that can result from implementing a dialogical writing classroom, as well as the complications of such a classroom.

To some degree, all learners have a desire to pry into understanding who they are, why they behave as they do, and where they might be heading in their lives. Her mere membership in the mainstream culture of power does not make Ashley immune from the vagaries of life. She could, no doubt, write of family issues or personal complexities that leave her confused and perplexed. How might she wonder about the ways that, as a woman, her opportunities might be diminished? On the other hand, what would it mean for Ashley to call her socioeconomic privilege into question? She, like anyone, would benefit from a more systematic and intentional means for reflection and action that would help her make better sense of who she is in the many social worlds she encounters.

However, as Africana philosopher Lewis Gordon (2000) argued, those whose lives are more marginalized from mainstream access to power and status have even greater needs to make meaning of what can only be construed as the absurdities of racism, classism, homophobia, and other socially constructed societal sifting mechanisms. Accordingly, it benefits such students to view literacy in general and writing in particular as means for making sense of their lives, as well as means for continuing to dialogue with mainstream culture. And, in the end, all classrooms, no matter where they are located, are populated by students who, for a multitude of factors, find themselves relegated to the sidelines. Six-figure salaries and four-bed-room houses don't preclude sexual abuse, rank prejudice, feelings of loss, worries of low self-esteem, and the like from occurring and, in some cases, may even exacerbate or mask such incidents.

What Is a Dialogical Classroom?

To answer the question posed in the heading of this section, my first response is to suggest that you should just be patient and read the book. It will eventually become clear. Still, I understand the need for and the practicality of a working definition, something we can attach to understandings already present in our cosmos and to which we can attach future understandings.

For the purposes of this book, a dialogical classroom is one in which literacy is used to immerse teacher and students in an ongoing reflective conversation with the texts of their lives. Let me unpack that. When I write *literacy is used to immerse teacher and students*, I'm urging those of us who teach to get in over our heads with explorations into who we are becoming, and that reading, writing, speaking, and listening be the means for doing so. We need to bring our expertise to these explorations, but we also need to bring our sense of wonder, so that we might value the expertise of our students and open ourselves to the dialogue. The liberal educator Paulo Freire (1970) reminded us that no dialogue can begin with the premise that some chosen among us can enter that dialogue, or that some voices carry more weight than others. So, to immerse is to expect all to go deep and take part in constructing new understandings, to blur and reinvent the definitions of teacher and student.

> A dialogical classroom is one in which literacy is used to immerse teacher and students in an ongoing reflective conversation with the texts of their lives.

Then what do I mean by *an ongoing reflective conversation*? As readers and writers of text, we author a response. A shrug, a sentence, a formal essay, a class discussion, a full-scale production with puppets are all responses. The Russian literary and language theorist Mikhail Bakhtin (1981) claimed that all understanding is merged with response, and that through response comes meaning—a restless, transient, ephemeral meaning that is contingent on context and inclined toward its next response. As he noted, "The relation to *meaning* is always dialogic. Even understanding itself is dialogic" (1986, p. 121, italics in the original).

Therefore, the conversation is not only reflective, it is ongoing; it exists over time. What occurs at the start of class pertains to that which ends it. Literature the dialogic classroom) across time and space ⫶

read in October is overtly connected to readings in March. What is written in brief one day can be extended a week later and added into a longer piece later in the month. Thoughts occurring in English class intersect with those from other subject areas. The dialogical classroom becomes unbounded and exists across time as well as space.

And always, we respond to text, or what I've called *the texts of our lives*. For me, what counts as text here begins with traditional print text, but also opens into electronic media, music, art, and other sensual stimuli. A pebble made smooth by the flow of a river, if you know how to read it, is as much a text as *A Tale of Two Cities*. The distant look in the eyes of your partner as the two of you try to untangle a relationship issue communicates meaning. The painting by Rousseau in which a couple in carnival garb emerges from the bare forest as the winter moon rises says one thing to me and, perhaps, something else to you. My dog, standing near where his treats are kept and staring bullets through my head, is trying to tell me something, if only I would interpret his actions as he intends. The blinking cursor and the doubt I feel as I ponder the next line . . .

As readers and writers, we are creators of texts, argues Louise Rosenblatt (1995). Doing so is an existential act. In creating text, students engage in what Bakhtin (1981) has called a "process of becoming," an ongoing dialogue with themselves and others in an attempt to make personal understandings of the contexts of their lives. All texts, the ones we read and the ones we write, become, to at least some degree, our texts. We take at least partial ownership of text, there being as many interpretations as there are readers (Rosenblatt, 1995).

There is a scene in the film *Saturday Night Fever* in which Stephanie, Tony's dancing partner, is gushing over the Franco Zeffirelli film production of *Romeo and Juliet*. "Oh yeah," says Tony, in recognition, "Shakespeare." Stephanie shakes her head. "No, Zeffirelli." The scene is played as a joke on Stephanie, but, in some ways, her response illustrates what both Rosenblatt (1995) and Bakhtin (1981) argued. True, Shakespeare originally wrote the play, but he adapted it from earlier sources. When Zeffirelli made his film, he freely interpreted Shakespeare's text in ways that were different from, say, the earlier George Cukor version or the more recent production by Baz Luhrmann. So it becomes Zeffirelli's *Romeo and Juliet*, or Stephanie's, or yours. Yet the text also always remains, at least in part, Shakespeare's.

Based on this working definition, I argue that all classrooms are dialogical; that they fit somewhere on a continuum between *completely dialogical* and *completely monological*, but never reach either limit. They can, however, skew in either direction. The less that educators recognize the dialogical possibilities and the less they create opportunities for multiple perspectives to be heard and considered, the more their classrooms will remain shifted toward the monological end of the scale. If teachers lecture in pronouncements, proclamations, and absolutes—if they never, at some point, say to a student, "That's an interesting way to think about it that never occurred to me"—then whatever dialogical sparks that exist in that room will find no tinder to ignite. A classroom that is driven by recitation of information instead of exploration of questions will, in the words of Bakhtin (1986), seem "meaningless to us; it is removed from dialogue" (p. 145).

A Working Definition of Dialogical Writing

When I began writing this book, teachers I worked with through the Red Clay Writing Project asked me what I meant by *dialogical writing*. I'm glad they asked, because as much as I hate to be pinned down on such things, I also knew that I needed to clarify for myself and others what such writing entails. Writing it down, I knew, was the means to compel me to bring some form to thoughts I allowed to roam a bit too freely in my head. I didn't necessarily want to break my wild horse thoughts—to define them into meaninglessness—but I did want to do more to fence in their grazing land.

In doing so, I created what I continue to call a working definition of dialogical writing. Even though at some point this definition will be frozen in time by the limitations of print-based media, I offer it as only a dialogue starter. What in this definition speaks to you? What would you add, drop, reorder, amend? How might this definition work in one situation and not another? And I reserve the right to continue to work this definition to fit my own ever-changing contexts.

To start, *dialogical writing represents an intersection of academic and personal* *writing*. Barbara Kamler (2001), an educator working in Australia, writes about the need to relocate the personal. She has argued, and I agree, that much of the writing done in school is either too exclusively personal or much too devoid of personality. An example of the overemphasis on the personal is the classroom in which students write tons of journals, but rarely are encouraged to revise those journals into more easily shared writing. Her concern is that although students might gain much experience in expressing their lives through writing, they gain little sense of how to craft and use those thoughts so that others can more readily find relevancy.

The other pendulum extreme, however, is marked by the seeming insistence that nothing of the experience, emotions, and biases of the writer enters into the finished product. Although columnists such as Maureen Dowd, Thomas Friedman, and Paul Krugman, all of whom

> **Dialogical writing . . .**
>
> - represents an intersection of academic and personal writing.
>
> - allows writers to bring multiple voices to the work.
>
> - involves thought, reflection, and engagement across time and is located in space.
>
> - creates opportunities for substantive and ongoing meaning making.

write for the *New York Times*, continue to affect public opinion through op-ed pieces brimming with personality, many English teachers insist that student writers vacuum all vestiges of self from their writing. Kamler (2001) argues that it is not one or the other. Instead, teachers need to help students see how their personal writing benefits from academic structures and how writing that is more academic in intent can benefit from the life and spirit of the personal.

In addition to being personal and academic, *dialogical writing allows writers to bring multiple voices to the work*. Those multiple voices are both within and without the writer. Kamler (2001) also writes about being wary of the term *voice*, as in "students need to find their voice." Two points in that phrase concern her. The first is that voice is set up as a kind of treasure hunt, something whole to be discovered instead of something in the process of creation. The singularity of voice also troubles her. Instead, she argues that we have many voices—for example, sister, child of divorced parents, experimenter with sexual lifestyles, comic book collector—and all of them are changing through dialogue over time. We need ways for all of those voices to come to the surface and not necessarily all in turn.

At the same time, we need our multiple voices within to engage with the multiple voices in our immediate and distant physical worlds. Our texts must be written in response to other texts, to which others will respond and we will remain in dialogue. Multiple and many forms of feedback and engagement should occur. Students writing to authors and characters; to younger students in other grades; in response to one another; in dialogue via online discussion forums; through multi-genre formats; on classroom wikis; in reaction to film, art, and music are all experiences that allow students to see writing as more than a singular self writing solely to the teacher as a requirement for a grade. And the more that we can coax diverse response, the more able we might be to see our work through the eyes of others.

A third aspect of dialogical writing is that it represents thought, reflection, and engagement across time and is located in space. Bakhtin (1981) reminds us that all meaning is contextual; our understandings depend on our experiences to date and the current experience as it anticipates future experience. Here's a quick example of what I mean. On a ride home from a beach weekend, I passed a hand-painted sign with the word *Stop* on one line and the word *Peaches* below it. Given that there was a roadside stand just up the highway, the context seemed to indicate that the sign was imploring us to pull over and check out the fruit. But a plum grower who felt that peach farmers were stealing his business might pass that spot and see himself as part of a growing movement to curtail peach production. The sign could also give insight into a personal drama in which one family member had left a roadside note to another family member to restrain their relative who everyone called "Peaches." And, of course, for want of a comma, the sign could even be a plea to Peaches herself.

No doubt, other contexts could be imagined. But the point is that the words are meaningless without context. And that context is more than a physical place—a room, a country, a planet—it is also a place in time. It has a remembered history, a contemplated now, and an anticipated future. Therefore, when we write dialogically, we engage with our thoughts while keeping those many interconnected contexts in mind. We must also be aware that our contexts will engage the fluid contexts of every reader of our work.

The only way to maintain this engagement is to see our writing as interconnected. The writing I jot today feeds my writing tomorrow, which nourishes or perhaps inhibits my work on a third day. As such, lower-stake, more tentative, and more frequent writing experiences (e.g., journals, freewrites) merge into higher-stake, more polished responses (e.g., blog entries, draft essays) that then result in more cumulative, more refined, and accomplished pieces (e.g., multigenre compositions, op-ed columns, interactive websites). Another way to think about the connectedness of text is to understand how reading and writing across genres can benefit all attempts at writing, no matter the genre. For example, I may not ever publish a poem, but I routinely write them because the effort nourishes and gives me insight into my prose. The intent is to keep my mesh of writing experience strengthening as it expands.

Finally, *the reflection, the multiple perspectives, and the engagement through context create opportunities for substantive and ongoing meaning making.* Writers come to understand how to use their writing to make multiple meaning of text, of issues, of themselves, of the world around them. Just as all classrooms have dialogical potential, all writing can help us make meaning of our lives. Most of us would imagine that a grocery list might not hold much spark to have us consider our existential condition. But given the right context—perhaps you've recently endured the sudden death of a close friend who died young and tragically—that routinized activity might help you understand the need to do the commonplace to see you through hard times, or it might help you realize that you've spent too much time on rote activities and need to shake up your life. Whatever the case, seeing writing as a dialogical act from which meaning is generated is what enables such an insight to occur.

What a Dialogical Writing Assignment Might Look Like

To be in dialogue, then, is to multitask. Bakhtin (1986) likens it to a drama with three characters: the self, the listener, and the larger society. My writing is a response to my general or some explicit experience. Take that tired old writing assignment, *What I did on my summer vacation.* If I were a student faced with responding to that prompt, I'd have to take several factors under consideration.

Among other things, I would need to connect to my understanding of vacations, what vacations look like in my family, what happened on my most recent vacation, and, specifically, what aspects of that I wanted to share. So the writing begins both from within and without the writer. As I write, I should be aware of what my writing reveals to me and to my reader about me and us. Why did I write so much about body surfing and not a word about dropping my dad's iPod in the sand, or vice versa?

Although my immediate reader might be the teacher, I, too, am a reader, and so is the larger society outside the classroom, although that connection is often, even for older students, difficult to grasp. My vacation essay connects to the many vacation essays written before and presages those to come. If, in my writing about that trip to the beach, I come to understand that the time spent there was really bittersweet or that sitting on the beach reading a book was more the highlight than riding waves, I have entered into a dialogue with myself, my direct audience, and the more indirect larger culture. I have now contributed to what we know and understand about summer vacations.

However, if the teacher does little or nothing to enhance the dialogic opportunities of the assignment, I am less likely to do all of the above consciously and with intent. If, at 9:30 on a Monday morning at the start of September, the teacher asks me to put away my math homework, take out my three-ring binder, and write five paragraphs about what I did last summer, I am very unlikely to enter into much dialogue with myself, the teacher, and, least of all, the community outside the school. No context has been created for dialogue, so therefore no expectation of dialogue exists. More important, if this is how most writing has been contextualized in my education, then writing as a tool for reflective dialogue has been stolen from me, if it was ever mine to have in the first place. On top of all of this, if I spent summer vacation taking care of my three-year-old brother while most of my classmates traveled the United States and abroad, there's a good chance I won't feel connected to the assignment.

But consider another scenario. My teacher has raised this overarching question for the year: *What happens when we, or circumstances, interrupt our daily routines?* The class, as a group, has decided that, for the first few weeks, we'll focus on the way summer vacation interrupts the routine of school. In particular, we want to know what might be useful and what might be problematic about having time away from the rigors of school.

For a few class meetings in a row, we've been writing, sharing, and discussing—online and face-to-face—short bursts of writing about vacations that went bust, ones that surprised us, dream vacations, stay-at-home vacations, and the like. At the same time we've read fiction, nonfiction, and poetry devoted to taking time away, charting as we did what they told us about breaking routine. We've also been exploring and then experimenting with the genres we've read, building on the shorter impromptu pieces. After a couple or three weeks, my teacher asks each of us to reflect upon what we've done by rereading not only what we've written, but also some of what others in class have shared. As we're reading, we're writing notes in margins or on sticky notes as we rediscover ideas that stand out to us, that make us think. Finally, we're told to develop an essay that's an argument about vacations and that springs from aspects of our accumulated work. After careful consideration of a few themes I've identified in my work, I decide to write about how not going to camp separates me from many of my friends, and how that decision by my parents—one predicated on short finances—has both disappointments and hidden rewards.

Back again in my role as teacher educator, I purposely chose to play with this shopworn assignment just to show that it's not the assignment, but the context that allows for greater possibilities for dialogical exploration. Given the context of questions and investigations into other texts, the theme, *How I spent my vacation*, takes on complexity and nuance. It also allows me to write about socioeconomic class issues in a way that is neither superficially frosted over nor one-sidedly moribund. Instead of reporting in a repetitious "and next" style, my writing about my summer becomes an exploration into that experience. It becomes a living conversation with myself as well as others.

What to Expect

What I've written is just a taste of where this book is going. Better yet, unlike the vacation writing assignment—which I fabricated solely for this chapter but really would like to try—the remainder of the examples will be taken from classrooms of teachers who are engaged in a dialogue with their practices. Although I certainly admire them and they're justifiably proud of what they've accomplished to date, neither they nor I want you to see their examples as best practice.

In a dialogical classroom, practice is always subject to context and is forever in a state of becoming. Therefore, what the teachers share here is practice—messy, complex, thoughtful, inspired, limited, and full of potential. It is offered for the dialogue it will stimulate. It is suggested with the full understanding that it could be done differently. It is practice that we hope will be adapted and not adopted. It is one possibility among many.

the nature of dialogical writing

My intent in this chapter has been to raise questions about and give tentative insights into the nature of dialogical writing. I have given you a taste of the opportunities and complexities of teaching writing from a dialogical stance. But it's only a taste. In Chapter 2, I address concerns that teachers frequently raise about enacting dialogical classrooms. Although I give credence to these legitimate issues,

I also argue for how we can develop means to move past them. Within this discussion, I highlight the principles and research that drive this work, as well as how all this connects to belief statements about writing developed by the National Council of Teachers of English (NCTE).

The next chapter is the first of three that illustrate what a dialogical stance on the teaching of writing might look like. This chapter asks what ways of thinking about and viewing classrooms do teachers need to develop to foster dialogue there. My concern is that, unless we as educators develop perspectives and ways of knowing that support dialogue, all other discussion on the subject is moot. To help readers cultivate these perspectives, I have coupled anecdotes from classrooms with discussions of the work of theorists, such as Rosenblatt, Freire, Bakhtin, Kamler, and Hermans and Kempen, whose work underpins taking a dialogical stance. The intent is to have the anecdotes animate the theory.

In Chapter 4, the focus is more attuned to the nuts and bolts of a dialogical classroom. Given what we know about the perspectives needed to create a dialogical space, what does this look like in terms of helping students learn about themselves while they also learn to craft their writing skills? Again, classroom anecdotes drive the discussion of the range of possible dialogic approaches. To better show the many facets of dialogical writing instruction, I've culled seven examples from a range of secondary classrooms, many of which are taught by teachers who have had substantive experience with the National Writing Project. Particularly in this chapter, I describe successful dialogical projects that can be done in a few days or no more than two or three weeks.

Chapter 5 describes five extended dialogical projects and specifically sketches the ongoing dialogue between curriculum, teaching, and assessment that exists in literacy classrooms. In particular, I argue that some forms of assessment—for example, portfolios, multigenre projects, self-selected projects—foster an assessment process that is more dialogical than more traditional, one-off kinds of assessments. Additionally, a dialogical assessment process is one that is educative and invites the learner to play a more active role, thus seizing some of the power and responsibility that accompanies assessment.

The last chapter of the book has two purposes. The first is to discuss the implications

Questions You Might Ask Yourself

- What does dialogue look like in a literacy classroom?

- What might teachers need to do and what perspectives might they need to cultivate to have their writing pedagogy better support a dialogical stance?

- How can an emphasis on dialogical writing enable students, whom school has marginalized, to feel that they and their cultures are more welcomed there?

- In what ways would a dialogical stance be crucial in an educational world in which too much writing practice seems driven by test scores and standardization?

- If I start to dialogue more with my students, will this open me to dialogical opportunities with colleagues, parents, and other educational stakeholders?

of this work: What does it mean for teachers, teacher educators, students, parents, administrators, and policymakers? Part of this discussion is the "so what" of taking a dialogical stance, but part of it is to provide all stakeholders with the responsibility and possible tools for engaging dialogue on the issues. The second purpose of this chapter is to remind readers of the existential and immediate need for this work and to argue that teaching writing in formulized ways for out-of-context, standardized writing tests hurts students, the teaching process, and, ultimately, our society. It's my belief that the negative effects of narrow views of literacy, and how it should be taught, get doubled and tripled for students whom school and society has marginalized. We need to conceive and implement better ways, and we need to do so now.

like planning.

I follow the chapters with two short bibliographical essays, both of which are intended to jump-start further reading about writing and writing classrooms. The first of these essays highlights books by writers reflecting on the writing process and includes reflections on their craft and art by writers as diverse as Flannery O'Connor and Eve Ensler, to name but two. The second bibliographical essay showcases books on the teaching of writing that I feel are worth the time tracking down, no matter what grade level you teach. For example, I discuss texts by Katie Wood Ray and George Hillocks, despite the fact that the former is focused on elementary students and the latter on adolescents. What matters most is that both books will inform your practice and enhance the writing of your students.

All of which leads us back to Ashley. If I think that she is cheating me and cheating herself by not engaging earnestly, intellectually, and emotionally in her writing for my course, I have to do more than blame her, blame all her former teachers, and/or blame a permissive society. I have to take responsibility. I have to engage her in dialogue about the content of the course and about the possibilities of developing understanding through writing. Maybe Ashley needs to do more to see and use writing as a dialogical act, but then, so do I. And that's what the rest of the book seeks to do: provide the wherewithal to rethink our writing classrooms as dialogical spaces.

writing as a dialogical act.

Chapter Two

The Whys of a Dialogical Classroom

Kevin Mink, as I'm writing this, is a master's level preservice teacher. As he works his way through his degree, he sends me sporadic and just a tad off-center emails to keep me updated on his progress. In a postscript to the latest, he writes: "Think it's any easier to be Brian Schultz, c. 2009, than B. Fecho?"

That was pretty cryptic, even for Mink, so I asked for clarification. After favorably comparing my work with Schultz's (2008) *Spectacular Things Happen along the Way*, Kevin went on to write that when he and another graduate student had read *Is This English?* (Fecho, 2004), they wondered, "Could Bob pull this off in GA, in 2009?" In other words, could I apply the dialogical teaching I had done some fifteen years earlier in a large, comprehensive high school in Philadelphia to classrooms in contemporary rural and suburban Georgia? Could students and teachers dialogue within the limitations of imposed standards, decontextualized assessments, and paced curricula, not to mention burgeoning technologies and media?

Not content to stop there—he rarely ever is—Mink then wondered not just if, but for how long. Giving me the benefit of the doubt that I could make a dialogical classroom happen, Kevin asked, "Can one pull this kind of thing off for any significant length of time?" He quoted radical journalist Andrew Kopkind (1995), who wrote, "In the windmill-tilting racket, the tilt is all; no one wants—or expects—the blades to stop" (p. 97). And then Kevin finished with his own point: "Yet Quixote took a beating, brother. Could he take it till retirement?"

Now you see why I like to teach, and why I particularly like to do it from a dialogical stance. Students such as Kevin—and throughout my high school and college teaching, I've had many—won't let me rest on my chalk dust. They push me. They dig down and ask the hard questions. And when they pose a tough query, they ask it of themselves as well. Giving life to a question is the first step in giving breath to a response.

[handwritten note in right margin: opposite of the dialogical classroom = the unengaged classroom]

Mink and his peers want to believe in the dialogical classroom because they dread the alternative. They have lived the unengaged classroom. They have been the victims of soul-deadening classes in which much of nothing is done; in which knowledge is thought to be a sacred torch passed to new generations; and in which little, if anything, is ever called into question. They have been drained as students by seemingly endless testing cycles and routinized lessons. They know what it's like to be told to leave their languages, cultures, and experiences hanging on a peg at the classroom door. They have been too often taught by teachers who believed that, in feeding their charges enough alphabet soup, those learners would regurgitate major works of world literature.

There is a Zen saying that I loosely remember this way: You cannot push the river. Teachers, particularly those new to teaching, see the established teaching structures of many schools and feel as if they are waist deep in a swift mountain stream, trying to get it to reverse course. What usually happens in such instances is that either the river sweeps past, basically ignoring them in its headlong rush to complete its mission, or it knocks them down and carries them away and they become the river. And so doubt leaks in.

To some teachers, dialogical teaching feels counterintuitive, as if they've decided to avoid crashing their car into a brick wall by stepping on the gas and pointing right at the obstacle. Then, too, modern classrooms often feel like spaces where there is too little time and too much to do. Part of that workload involves increased standardized testing. Teachers in some districts here in Georgia tell me that up to one-sixth of their total school days is spent administering

Fears That Limit Dialogical Teaching

- Fear of doing the wrong thing

- Fear that students will perform poorly on standardized tests

- Fear that there is too much to do and too little time

- Fear of spinning out of control

- Fear that students aren't up to the task

tests that are imposed from outside their classrooms. With testing comes increased surveillance. Given so much scrutiny, teachers worry that a dialogical stance will lead to discussions of subject matter that some parents or politicians or even students might feel would be better left outside the classroom. And, given the pathological nature of schools where testing creates an atmosphere of inability, a few too many teachers give in to the concept that "these students" can't handle work that invites them to think in critical and informed ways.

As a university professor, I know how this institution, on record as being committed to ideals of academic freedom, gets in the way of my teaching through structures that enable lecture while constricting engagement. Therefore, it's no great leap for me to understand how the policies of public schools could serve more as obstacles rather than as means of facilitation. And the bureaucratic policies of the urban school district, where I taught for more than twenty years, remain vivid and present in my memory. Besides, old friends who still teach there and new friends who teach in the many schools around UGA fill my head with tales of initiatives and mandates that continually shave away at what little is left of teacher autonomy.

So I understand that the concerns are complicated and real. In fact, if we were having this discussion in my classroom, my first response would be to engage us in an exploration of issues and obstacles. What, I would ask, gets in the way of our ability to teach in dialogical ways? If most, and perhaps all, of us in the room acknowledge that taking a dialogical stance is how we would like to teach, why don't we then teach like that more often, with more substance, to greater effect?

Here, as in my classroom, it's key that I don't let this discussion become a faculty room gripe session. If we have issues, what are the issues, but, more important, if we believe in the approach, how do we work past the issues? In the remainder of this chapter, I acknowledge and explore concerns most frequently expressed to me about enacting a dialogical stance in a literacy classroom. Within this discussion, I invoke theory, research, and experience that argue for using dialogical practices in classrooms despite and, in many cases, because of the obstacles placed in the path of such teaching. In particular, I show how the belief statements authored by the National Council of Teachers of English provide a sound foundation upon which to base such arguments.

Countering Fears with Substantive Beliefs

If given the time and space, I could easily argue that creating a writing classroom based on dialogical principles supports all eleven statements in *NCTE Beliefs about the Teaching of Writing* (see p. xi). But that would be overkill and would run the risk of diluting what I consider to be the key ways a dialogical stance on writing animates,

indeed, invigorates these beliefs. I certainly believe that dialogical practice acknowledges that everyone has the capacity to write, that we do so for many purposes, that
conventions of writing play an important role in the process, and that talk and writing intersect in complicated ways. I also agree that new technologies and a range of
modalities influence our writing, and that we assess that writing in ways both complex and compassionate. Allusions to these beliefs will flitter somewhat tacitly, but
nonetheless consistently, through this text.

    However, it's the remaining five beliefs—*that writing is a process, that it's also
a tool for thinking, that it springs from complicated social relationships, that it's intimately
connected to reading, and that it's learned by doing*—that will garner most of my attention, both here and in the remaining chapters. But particularly for the next few
pages, I will use these five beliefs to provide a response to the very real fears and
concerns expressed by teachers who genuinely contemplate that upstream walk into
a dialogical classroom. I hope to suggest a perspective that makes the effort both
plausible and worthwhile.

Fear of Doing the Wrong Thing/Seeing Writing as a Process

Most teachers want to teach well and do right by their students. When faced with
teaching in such an ethos of standardization, many teachers see direct, atomized
instruction—focusing on discrete skills coupled to decontextualized drill—as the
intuitive approach. The test, they surmise, covers cause and effect, so doing cause-
and-effect exercises seems to make sense. What seems counterintuitive to them is
taking a more contextual and holistic dialogical approach, one in which discussing
cause and effect would be embedded in inquiry-based projects that involved much
reading, writing, speaking, and listening. They worry that understanding the ways
cause and effect play out in reading and writing will be lost in the complexity of the
inquiry.

    Penn Jillette (2009), the taller, talkative half of the magicians Penn and
Teller, in a discussion of President Obama's recession initiatives, argued that often
what feels counterintuitive is actually what needs to be done. He cites driving on
slippery roads and, as only he might, fire-eating as examples of his point. In the
former, Penn reminds us that drivers need to turn into the direction of a skid, an
action that, at least to most of our sensory organs, seems suicidal. In other words,
if my car is skidding to the right, I should actually turn that way. To many drivers,
that action seems scary—to drive toward the direction in which they're losing control. But it is, indeed, the right thing to do because the maneuver will get the front
tires once again in line with the back tires and allow you to go straight. Turning
away from the direction of the skid will just enhance the car's ability to complete
one or several 360-degree spins.

NCTE Belief Statements about Teaching Writing

Focus beliefs for this book:

Writing . . .

is a process

is a tool for thinking

involves complicated social relationships

is connected to reading

is learned through the act of writing

Penn also argues that fire-eaters have to overcome the natural inclination to rip the torch from their mouth when it threatens to burn them. Instead, they have to trust that the moistness of the mouth and the removal of oxygen will kill the fire. So instead of pulling the torch away, fire-eaters actually push it further in and close their lips around the flames, effectively stifling them. From where I stand, just putting a flaming torch into your mouth in the first place seems counterintuitive. I'll trust Penn on how best to douse it.

And, in the end, it's about trust—specifically, trust in the mentor—that can help us to take a counterintuitive approach. In the case of Penn Jillette, his father took him out to an empty parking lot and had him practice skid avoidance over and over. Before attempting to do so himself, Penn repeatedly watched his carny mentor extinguish a flaming torch by pursing his lips around it. Through watching people he trusted successfully execute the counterintuitive maneuver, he was able to imagine himself doing the same.

I'm not sure you know me well enough to trust me, but I'll wade into that stream nonetheless. In doing so, I want to introduce you to some of my research mentors and discuss the ideas of these people I came to trust. The hope is that our combined experiences might help you at least get your toes wet in terms of dialogical practice.

writing as a process

I came of age as a teacher when Janet Emig (1971), Donald Graves (1983), Peter Elbow (1981), and Donald Murray (1997) were arguing that writing was a process. It's not an accident that Victor Villanueva (1997) begins his retrospective on writing scholarship with a section on what he calls a "'given' in our conversations"—that writing is a process. To acknowledge writing as a process, as Murray (1997) suggests, is to respond to the work of students "not for what they have done, but for what they may do; not for what they have produced, but for what they may produce" (p. 6).

These beliefs connect to what Bakhtin (1981) meant when he argued that all meaning comes through response and that response remains suspended between the past and the future. We can't write anything that doesn't spring from what we already have knowledge of, even as it positions us for future response. Although it wasn't widely acknowledged at the time—because much of this initial work on process writing preceded his introduction into Western thought—Bakhtin's work resonates with the concept that writing is not a discrete act aimed at producing a singular product. Instead, all that we write is part of a mesh of responses that simultaneously connects us to what we have come to understand while raising future questions and pointing toward other possibilities. Even something as pedestrian as a grocery list begins with what was left off the last list and leaves space, intended or unintended, for future lists. Each list is part of an ongoing dialogue in the process of writing.

Whether we as educators acknowledge this process, it occurs without us. However, when we try to teach writing by taking it apart and addressing subskill after subskill, it's tantamount to turning away from the skid. It might, on some surface level, seem right, but it undermines the whole intent of seeing writing as an ongoing process. Such an approach sacrifices complex fluency and engagement in a meaning-making process for minimal proficiency on a small aspect of the whole. To me, having students focus too early and too long on punctuation, spelling, and all of the many conventions that lead up to the exercise of writing is problematic. Doing so is like disassembling an entire car and asking novice drivers to rebuild it before they can get behind the wheel. Most would lose all interest and sense of purpose in driving long before the machine was put back together.

When we stand in front of or among students, we have to imagine that the teaching of writing is like throwing our classroom into a skid. The pressures of the context—students doing well on standardized tests, legislators holding our schools' destinies in their hands, the cost of all those prep books and testing materials—impel us to avoid the crash and burn by turning away from the skid. I'm asking you to trust my experience as an urban high school teacher and teacher educator, the experiences of well-respected writers and writing researchers, and, not at all the least, the experiences of the writing teachers outlined later in this book. We urge you to turn into the skid; enacting a dialogical practice will get the wheels of your classroom back where they belong and keep the writing process moving forward. You still might be negotiating slick surfaces, but you'll feel more confident in your ability to do so.

Fear That Students Will Perform Poorly on Standardized Tests/Seeing Writing as a Tool for Thinking

In the first year of Crossroads, a small learning community (SLC) I helped to develop in a comprehensive high school in North Philadelphia, we had the opportunity to put many dialogical aspects of teaching into practice. Along with inquiries driven by overarching questions, class work that built on students' cultures and experiences, and scheduling that allowed teachers to spend more time with students, the faculty also expected students to be able to pose their own questions and generate their own ways of responding. Near the end of our first year of existence, the news division of NBC sent a producer and a film crew to document our efforts as part of an hour-long special report on progressive education.

During the three weeks they were with us, then-news anchor Tom Brokaw spent a day at the school interviewing faculty and students. At one point he asked the three of us who first conceived the SLC if we thought our students could compete with students who he suggested were getting less process learning but more of a fact base. The videotape shows me answering with confidence that yes, our students could compete because they knew how to make meaning of information and how to search out their own answers.

No one could ever confuse me with someone who is deeply religious. Thus that response to Tom Brokaw remains one of my greatest leaps of faith. At the time, I had little evidence to back up my claim, just the belief that the way we were teaching through the exploration of questions allowed students to become experienced and proficient at seeking their own understandings. Instead of just accepting information without question or spouting opinion without developing strong evidence, we were encouraging students to interrogate their own stances as well as that of others. Doing so, we felt, we were helping students to be better able to negotiate academics and life.

But at the moment of my response, it was pure faith that I was expressing. Only later, as the SLC matured, did we start to see the evidence that our students not only could get into universities, tech schools, and the military, but they also knew how to problem solve setbacks and move with steady progress toward achieving graduation, promotion, or employment. Their scores on standardized tests and college entrance examinations improved; more students entered college who would not have done so otherwise; and more students stayed to graduate. The websites of the Coalition of Essential Schools (http://www.essentialschools.org/) and the Institute for Student Achievement (http://www.studentachievement.org/), two organizations committed to SLCs and inquiry-based learning, bear out our results on a broader scale.

It distresses me that some teachers with whom I come in contact draw a line between success on standardized tests and dialogical practice, as if the two were mutually exclusive. That's really not the case if you consider what dialogical practice asks of students and teachers, particularly what it asks of writers and writing. Again, going back to some of the milestone work in composition studies, cognitive psychologists, such as Linda Flower (1981), have long argued that writing is a complex, problem-solving activity. Each writing activity, from a to-do list to an epic novel, requires writers to determine to whom they are writing, with what purpose, to what length, through what means, with what tone, and other such considerations. As the process evolves, writers must assess such aspects of their work as where their writing is taking them, is it holding together, should ideas be added or left off, or will this capture a reader's attention. If this problem posing is called to the surface, young writers begin to see that writing is both a treasure trove and a burden of choice and responsibility.

Educators Ann Berthoff (1984), Ken Bruffee (1984), and Derrick Jensen (2004), among others, have argued that writing leads to dialogue that leads to the construction of meaning. Social and cognitive psychologists, such as Hubert Hermans and Harry Kempen (1993) and Crystal Park and Carol Joyce Blumberg (2002), echo these sentiments in their work with using writing in therapy situations. Content area specialists—Michael McKenna and Richard Robinson (2009) and Harvey Daniels, Steven Zemelman, and Nancy Steineke (2007), for example— have long held that writing and reading contribute to learning course material in subjects beyond the English classroom. This broad and deep body of work points to the understanding that, when given time to explore ideas and make meaning through writing, students develop a more grounded and complex understanding of themselves as learners. Such an understanding usually results in students excelling and prevailing in all aspects of school and education, not the least of which would be standardized writing assessments.

The typical state- or district-run writing assessment takes place during a discrete and usually short time period, frequently contained within a portion of a single school day. Generally students are given a choice from among a few prompts. The better assessments allow for some sort of prewriting/drafting stage. Upon completion, the assessments are most likely bundled off and scored holistically by paid scorers, although computer scoring is beginning to raise its controversial head.

The idea that such writing is frequently timed worries me less than the idea that these prompts are almost always disconnected from the ongoing lives of the students, and even the ongoing life of the classroom. Because many writing tasks must be done in a hurry—journalists and bloggers writing for deadline; emergency reports needed yesterday; entreaties for forgiveness for a bit of foolishness—I can live with the idea that at least some writing assessments should limit the time spent producing them. But asking students to write from a cold start on topics that seem to fall from the sky just invites surface-level responses. Remember the summer vacation essays in Chapter 1?

However, if we think about what abilities a standardized writing assessment calls for, we can see how the student who has been encouraged to embrace writing as a way to make and communicate meaning is at an advantage. Being able to view each writing task as a problem-solving venture and to have the wherewithal to assess the task at hand gives students an edge in such writing situations. Furthermore, these students have much practice at finding ways to personalize a writing task—to see the academic need, but also to write in meaningful ways for themselves. Having

experienced the understanding that comes through writing, they can take a decontextualized writing assessment and develop a motivation for completing it other
than some sense of academic responsibility or fear of punishment.

In readying myself to complete this book, I read through a number of texts
on writing that were sitting on my shelf. Perhaps famed writing teacher Brenda
Ueland (2007) summed up this concept of writing to make meaning best:

> I want to assure you with all earnestness that *no* writing is a waste of time. . . . With
> every sentence you write, you have learned something. It has done you good. It has
> stretched your understanding. I know that. Even if I knew for certain that I would
> never have anything published again, and would never make another cent from it, I
> would still keep on writing. (p. 14)

As teachers, we need to show our faith in the process. From writing comes meaning that identifies new questions, new reflection, and, ultimately, more writing.

Fear That There Is Too Much to Do and Too Little Time/Seeing How Reading and Writing Are Related

Of course, this is true. There IS too much to do and too little time. I won't waste
the effort trying to refute the irrefutable.

So what to do about that? One central tenet of the Coalition of Essential
Schools (2010) is *less is more*. Another way to think about it is to teach more about
fewer things. Reform educator Grant Wiggins (1989) put a different spin on this
perspective; he wrote of the futility of trying to teach everything of importance.
Consider how overgrown, cumbersome, and crowded curricula have become in the
twenty years since he wrote that article. No matter how you phrase it, the point is
that we have glutted curricula and textbooks to the extent they lose all effective-
ness. To try to teach it all, or even the bulk of what is required by most districts,
is akin to walking an egg past the stove in the hope of cooking it. The amount of
exposure needed to produce the result won't be nearly enough.

As educators, we need to find ways to streamline our practices. Given the
vast quantities of material available to be taught, and an ever-burgeoning list of
necessary skills for negotiating school and the world outside school, those of us
who work in education should strive for what I call seamlessness—the logical and
mutually supportive dialogue between all subject matter that we teach. Rather than
sprinkling disconnected and discrete lessons through the learning week, the various
subsets of our curriculum should speak to and resonate with one another. What
we do in vocabulary should feed our literature study that then enables our writing
practice, and this would further support presentations and media work and study
skills and so on. The limits of space make this preceding example seem far too

linear—starting with vocabulary was entirely random on my part—but the point is that the lines that divide this subject work should be blurred and in flux.

Understanding the significant connection between reading and writing is a substantive step toward seamlessness and enacting *less is more*. When we acknowledge the ways reading and writing mutually further understanding, we can better imagine how to integrate both into more classroom activities. By making reading and writing part of everyday knowledge construction, we not only get more education for our effort, but we also send messages to students that when we read, we write, and when we write, we read. All that, and it saves time.

Teachers examining their own classrooms have been especially curious about the ways reading and writing transact, perhaps taking their cue from *Breaking Ground: Teachers Relate Reading and Writing in the Elementary School* (Hansen, Newkirk, & Graves, 1985). This volume launched the publishing careers of some of the most recognized teacher-researchers: Nancie Atwell, Carol Avery, Ellen Blackburn (later Karelitz), Cora Lee Five, Jack Wilde, Susan Benedict, and Linda Rief. In an era when readiness exercises and handwriting dittos constituted the writing curriculum in many primary grades, these teacher-researchers showed through case studies and careful documentation of teaching and learning how learners connect reading and writing as they become literate.

While working with high school students in rural Alaska, another teacher-researcher, Tammy Van Wyhe (2000), investigated the ways her students transacted with poetry as readers and writers. What stands out in Van Wyhe's work are the multiple ways students embraced poetry as a part of their adolescent experience and how email exchanges with students in Lucille Rossbach's class in Colorado facilitated their growing involvement. For instance, discussions of poetry began to show up in hall talk, and poems, like pictures of teen idols, got taped to lockers. Van Wyhe even documented a visit to the school by a poet who participated in the email exchanges. Although it pressed them for time, players on the hockey team delayed travel to a game until they could meet their e-mentor in person.

Writing educators, such as Katie Wood Ray (1999) and George Hillocks (2007), have done substantive work in schools to remind us of the ways reading and writing support each other. Ray shows how a close study of the craft from established authors results in young writers developing a deeper and more complex understanding of how text is generated. By having students read in ways that make meaning not just of what authors write, but also of how they write, she takes advantage of the ways reading and writing remain in continual and intimate dialogue. That she does so with elementary learners should, in my mind, erase any arguments offered by secondary teachers that their students aren't up to the task.

Hillocks (2007) makes an eloquent argument for including more narrative writing in secondary English classes. Part of his argument recognizes that, in teaching writing or reading, we are, in effect, teaching both. What we learn about narrative through a close reading of examples informs how we approach narrative on the blank page, which further informs our future encounters with published narratives. He also reminds us of Judith Langer's (2001) work in schools where students from working-class and working-poor neighborhoods still excel academically. Langer identified the importance of bringing reading/writing connections to the surface in classrooms and of graphically discussing the ways reading and writing shape each other.

For me, embracing the reading/writing connections led to rethinking how I taught literature to students. No longer did I view it as my job to teach *Hamlet* or *Makes Me Wanna Holler*. Instead, it was my job to teach students how to read and respond to those and other texts. It's not a fine difference. To teach *Hamlet* is to see the text as the key component, as if understanding that specific text, its context, and how it was generated are of prime importance.

And such may be for some teachers. But for me, helping students develop skills for unpacking all text, and using writing as a means for doing so, carried much more motivational weight. Sure, *Hamlet* and *Makes Me Wanna Holler* are both meaty and vibrant texts, and I had good reasons for wanting students to specifically read those texts, but the intention wasn't so they would "know" those texts as one might "know" the earth is round. I saw both works as complex investigations of the human condition and wanted my students to have the opportunity to shape those texts in order to have the texts shape them. In ferreting out their own meaning, the students would become readers not just of *Hamlet* but of all texts.

What I'm discussing is what literary scholar Louise Rosenblatt (1994) described as transactional perspectives on reading and writing. As writers, we are generators of text; writing is a creative act. As we write, we enter into a transactional relationship with the text we are creating. That is, we shape the text to better convey our thoughts, but the text shapes us at the same time. This mutual shaping is more contextual and unpredictable than an interaction, the results of which are more regular and expected. It's the difference between heating water to 212 degrees and having it turn to steam and splashing cold water on strangers going by.

As the first readers of our own text, we are involved in a process of changing it even as we set the pixels in place on our monitors. Reading, like writing, is both transactional and generative. It is why some students find Holden Caulfield utterly fascinating and others see him as a total loser. We bring him, and all text, to our lives in different ways, and thus our lives are shaped differently by those texts. By understanding and acting upon the transactional aspects of both reading and writing, we can create opportunities in our classrooms for mutual exploration of each.

There will never be enough time and we really should never attempt to teach it all. Instead, we should grasp the possibilities presented by inherent connections in our subject matter. When we read, we write. When we write, we read. Each depends upon the other. Teaching from that stance moves our practice ever closer to being seamless.

Fear of Spinning Out of Control/Literate Practices Are Embedded in Complicated Social Relationships

classroom as dynamic transactiona

For me, one of the most fascinating aspects of classrooms is that they are dynamic, transactional spaces. As Pratt (1991) has indicated, classrooms are zones where languages and cultures cross borders and come into contact, where the many lives we live have the potential to mingle with the many lives of others. Gloria Anzaldúa (2007) has characterized such spaces as *la frontera*, the borderlands. It's here that language, culture, ways of knowing, and the like enter into dialogue and undergo mutual shaping. It's here where we encounter what I call *wobble*, that moment when some predictable and stable aspect of our belief system becomes less so. It starts to wobble and, in doing so, we must pay attention.

However, that free-flowing and somewhat unpredictable aspect of classrooms that so draws me in, frightens and repels others. As a result, many secondary English teachers don't open themselves to dialogical relationships. They worry that by validating students' personal searches for meaning, their own identities as teachers and the traditional culture of the classroom will spin out of their control and chaos will reign. Fearing this loss of control, teachers behave in ways that recognize only certain cultures and validate the identities of only certain students, primarily those who are White and come from homes that are comfortably centered socially, politically, and economically (Finn, 1999; Heath, 1983).

This need to exert control on classrooms extends way beyond teachers. State and federal policies have increasingly minimized teacher choice. The drive for standardization of assessment, curricula, and even dress are, as Jensen (2004) noted, initiatives "to make sure students meet a set of standardized criteria so they will later be able to fit into a world that is itself increasingly standardized" (p. 5). As a result, assessment that is mandated with little local input or interpretation drives curriculum and teaching, creating what Coles (2003) and Darling-Hammond (2004) have described as a narrow and primarily economic view of literacy.

Pressed to the wings of the educational stage, students who are marginalized for sociocultural factors, such as race, class, gender, and sexual identity, find it difficult to see themselves in the culture of school. Consequently, many opt out. For example, students in the United States living in low-income families are at approximately four times greater risk of dropping out of school than peers from high-income families (Laird, DeBell, & Chapman, 2006). Those low-income students who do physically stay in school all too frequently seem to opt out emotionally and intellectually.

At least for a large portion of his K–12 education, such was the case with Andy, a teen at a local high school here in Georgia who was self-described as a marginal student without much interest in reading. However, as he found himself entering the last semester of his senior year, Andy also found himself searching for a richer understanding of the gay lifestyle he was entering. In particular, his identity as a standout wrestler on the school team was in conflict with his identity as a gay teen with a boyfriend. Trying to resolve how to come out to friends and family while remaining true to his identity under construction created considerable emotional weight for him.

It was at this point that Andy entered the classroom of an English teacher he had never met until then—Kristi Amatucci, now a teacher educator. Taking advantage of a personal literacy memoir that Kristi had assigned early in the semester, Andy came out to her:

> Then came my junior year. A lot of important things happened to me. One was that I got my first car, the second is that I would be turning 18 soon, but the most important thing was that finally, I came out to my parents and family; I also met my boyfriend. During this time in my life I started to read more about gay culture. My favorite book of all time is *How I learned to snap.* . . . In the past I have considered myself to be a slow reader, but I finally figured out it was because I was reading things that were of no significance to me.

Simply noting in her journal that "It's gonna be an interesting semester," Kristi then set out to find ways to dialogue with Andy at a level of openness with which he felt comfortable.

Andy and Kristi, that early winter day, were poised for a dialogical relationship. In asking her students to write about their literate lives, Kristi presented an invitation for them to share facets of the many selves they were in the process of shaping. Taking Kristi at her word, Andy revealed aspects of his identity and a culture that he was only beginning to investigate for himself. Sensing that Andy was searching for an adult he could trust and understanding that he didn't seem to be in crisis, Kristi positioned herself as a sounding board as Andy, on his own initiative, used her assignments and his own reading choices to explore his sexual identity. Through the rest of the semester, they found ways to discuss, both on paper and face-to-face, the gay adolescent literature he was reading in an effort to clarify his vision of himself in the gay community.

As Andy gradually came out to more members of the school community, Kristi saw their personal dialogue as insight into her practice. Because no dialogue is a one-way street, Kristi became aware that the low-key, friend-to-friend conversations she had with Andy about his literature could be replicated within her larger classroom. As she wrote,

> I was forced to rethink several aspects of my approach toward teaching literature and composition. What is essential for students to know and do? How can my teaching goals be best met? How might the roles of teacher and student shift, making symmetrical relationships more the norm in high school classrooms? My relationship with Andy left me with these questions and more. How would I change as a teacher based on what I'd learned from Andy?

It might have been much easier for Kristi, early on in their teacher–student relationship, to send signals that she preferred to keep that relationship more focused on the classroom topics that she assigned. However, by engaging in dialogue, Andy and Kristi developed insights into identities they were and continue to be in the process of shaping. Although Andy and Kristi never enlarged their discussion to the level of whole-class participation—perhaps neither was ready to do so—both had come to see the power of letting complex social relations enter into dialogue in the English classroom.

At the start of this section, I offered the observation that many teachers fear a loss of control if they take a dialogical approach in the classroom. They accept, if not embrace, many centralized efforts at standardization because such efforts create a space where little variation in subject matter and response occurs. When the expectation for student response is primarily to give back information previously supplied by the teacher or a text, then classrooms maintain a certain pace and comfort for teachers beset by calls to teach and test with regularity and conformity. In this manner, teachers maintain control over students, principals maintain control over teachers, superintendents over principals, and so on.

To break this oppressive chain, I suggest that teachers spin out of control. Generally, the thought of spinning out of control seems like a bad thing to do. Only calamity, it is thought, can follow such an event. But perhaps the only way for teachers to escape the centralized and standardized curricula, pacing schedules, and assessments is to spin out of that control, somewhat like how a wide receiver might spin out of the grasp of a defensive back. Until we as educators see the ways response, and thus meaning, are controlled via centralized and standardized means, we can't imagine ways to open the dialogical possibilities of response and to spin in ways that set us free.

As Kristi and Andy illustrated, engaging in dialogical transactions allowed them to gain new insight in the respective identities they were building. For Andy, dialogical transactions with Kristi helped to enlarge his sense of self as a reader and writer as well as contribute to the deliberate construction of how he saw himself as a gay teen. In writing a final paper for Kristi, he responded to a Nadine Gordimer short story: "This just goes to show you what you lose when you let something like fear rule over you. . . . Anyone can see that if you let fear run your life, you can never be happy." So, too, Kristi's ongoing construction of herself as a literacy teacher was, at least to an extent, built upon her ongoing dialogical transactions with Andy and her willingness, like Andy, to show some gumption in pulling her practice away from the stultifying forces of standardization. This leaves me with a perhaps odd, but still fitting, question: Given the experiences of Andy and Kristi, why aren't more of us who educate spinning out of control, the better to engage our students in personal and meaningful, existential explorations?

Fear That Students Aren't Up to the Task/People Learn to Write by Writing

When I first began having high school students explore language as if they were linguistic ethnographers, other teachers told me that teens had no interest in language and that such research was beyond them. When Lisa Hall, a teacher you'll meet more fully later in the book, initiated dialogue journals in her classroom, she was told that her special education students would be unable to sustain them. When Georgia teacher Eric Hasty sought district permission to have his students investigate what it means to read books that are outside their cultural experience, he was told that it wouldn't improve adequate yearly progress. When Geoff Winikur, a high school teacher in Philadelphia, introduced *Rule of the Bone*, a book with complex and adult themes, to his working-class African American and Latino students, many outside his classroom imagined calamity and upheaval. Schools might not have all the resources they need, but at least some have naysayers aplenty.

How do we know what students can do until we ask them to do it? And, if they are not yet able, when do we start to teach them? How else will they learn? Why must it always be someone else's job?

We learn to write by writing. We become better writers when the writing we do springs from the riches, embarrassments, victories, tragedies, conundrums, concerns, delights, and, yes, even the routines of our lives. As Kamler (2001) noted, all writing must be filled with the many voices of our many selves just as it must also be filled with the many expectations of a literate society. The only way we can begin approaching fluency with such complexity is to write, write often, write in context, write with purpose, and write until the keys on our word processors become indistinguishable from one another.

Brenda Ueland (2007) wrote of the need to sit before a typewriter—she began her career in the 1930s—and be patient, but be ready. More bluntly, Mary

Pipher (2006) of *Reviving Ophelia* fame noted, "We [writers] learn to put our behinds in the chair and stay there" (p. 77). Science fiction writer Ray Bradbury (1996) acknowledged that writers need to fill their lives with experiences, but they also have to translate that experience into story by committing thought to paper. Given that Bradbury has more than 500 published works, we know where his behind has been. Flannery O'Connor (1979), in her take-no-prisoners way, declared, "Teaching any kind of writing is largely a matter of helping the student develop the habit of art" that, like any other habit, is cultivated "over a long period of time, by experience" (p. 101).

We who teach need to sit students down and give them daily and multiple opportunities to write. The task is too vital and complex for any other approach. Every moment young writers spend bubbling answers on a multiple-choice test is a moment taken from their writing experience. Editing text in a skill book is not writing, at least not of any consequence. Making verbs and nouns agree on a worksheet will most likely not enable verbs and nouns to agree in someone's writing. Creating paragraphs with a topic sentence, three sentences of support, and a conclusion robs precious time from writers who are trying to use writing as a way to make meaning of their lives. At the sacrifice of all rote seatwork, we must put students to the work of writing. Most will surprise us with what they generate. All will become better writers in the process.

I had a superintendent in Philadelphia with whom I rarely agreed. However, we did have one intersection of thought. He would say that it isn't enough for teachers to state that they believe students can generate and interpret complex text; teachers need to act like they believe it. Action must follow thought. We learn to write by writing. No matter how messy, labor intensive, and time consuming it might be, we need to let students continually muck with text. The question shouldn't be if they, the students, are up to the task; we should be asking, are we?

writing as a way to make sense of are life

Questions You Might Ask Yourself

- What are the fears that keep me from making my writing classroom more dialogical?

- What are the resources and support I might muster to help me work through my fears?

- What are some simple things I can do tomorrow to make the ideas found in the *NCTE Beliefs about the Teaching of Writing* more visible in my practice?

- What am I doing every day not to give in to the fears and replicate what research, theory, and common sense tell me is bad teaching?

Answering Kevin Mink

What I've done so far is, to an extent, artificial. You can't really pair off one fear with one NCTE belief statement. It doesn't work that way because the belief statements speak to and resonate with one another. Really there are multiple beliefs that argue why you should acknowledge your fear, but summon the strength and courage to work beyond it. The evidence is deep and wide and long.

I'd like to be able to write that I had something profound to say in response to Kevin's question about enacting a dialogical writing approach in a contemporary Georgia classroom. He was particularly concerned about how long someone can continue to buck the system. But my main response, in all its pedestrian glory, ran this way: "I'd like to think I could offer some adapted to the context form of what I did [in Philadelphia] and continue to perhaps get the blades [of the Quixote windmill] to pause and reconsider their direction." Just before I sent the email, I added this point: "But that's what I have you & others for: fresh tilters."

In many ways, my fuller response to Kevin is this book. With it, I've broadened my search for fresh tilters, one of whom is Russ Turpin, a teacher you'll learn more about in the next chapter. In reading a draft of this book, Russ responded by telling me via email that coping with furlough days, finishing a degree program, taking on new career responsibilities, and negotiating the myriad frictions that crop up daily in teaching had made this a hard year for him. Still, he persistently explored dialogical teaching and, despite some early ambivalence on the part of his students, he continued to "trust the process." His bulldog ways were rewarded as students completed an extensive reflective project—more on this in Chapter 5— that showed how deeply they had learned "about themselves, their worlds, tolerance, respecting others' opinions . . . all that good stuff."

He went on to write that "I guess my response to Mink might be—hell yes, this dialogical, inquiry-based approach can be sustained in a rural, southern, conservative, technologically deficient classroom." And perhaps with a bit too much modesty, he concluded,

> I don't intend to brag. It's not me; it's the pedagogical approach and the process. I have to be absolutely dedicated to that approach and process in order for "it" to work, and I can't be afraid to shift gears when it's necessary, but all of that, too, is part of the approach and the process. It just plain works if people will give it a try.

At least for Russ, the engagement and learning his dialogical efforts fostered were worth the doubt and uncertainty he encountered along the way.

David Thomas, who now teaches at the Harvard Business School, used to consult with small learning communities in Philadelphia on issues of group dynamics and institutional racism. As an African American, David was acutely aware of how schools have historically been used to oppress students from marginalized populations. He would ask teachers this question: Being part of such institutions, what are you doing every day not to replicate that oppression? So I turn the question to you. What are you doing every day not to give in to the fears by replicating what research, theory, and common sense tell us is bad teaching?

Here's your horse. Here's your lance. Saddle up.

Chapter Three

Developing Dialogical Perspectives

I believe that learning is not a safe act. If it were, I don't think we'd truly be learning. I try to promote an environment where students can enter and feel as though they are not judged for their comments or opinions, but I know that is not a given simply because I'd like for it to be. I cannot ensure a safe place for everyone in my room, but I try to have them understand they are always valued.

Angela Dean, the writer of this excerpt, teaches in a suburban high school in a large county within the Atlanta, Georgia, metro area. Later in this chapter, you'll learn more about Angela and where she teaches, but for now, just let her words settle into your consciousness. Take a moment to go back and read her thoughts. Think about what they tell you about her concept of teaching.

What perhaps strikes me most about what Angela wrote is how succinctly she got at the complexity of a classroom. My goodness, of course it's not safe, is it? Nor does wishing make it so. Although as teachers we might strive to make our classes less threatening, we know that we have only so much control over the context, and that threat can enter in unforeseen ways.

Angela acknowledges the limits of her influence to subdue threat, but counters by asserting her sincere attempts to have all students feel valued. Her hope is that by creating a space within which students can develop and express their voices, they will find ways to mutually work through whatever issues might arise. So she sets up a tension between her unifying attempts at valuing what students bring and their need to express themselves as individuals undergoing multiple and rapid identity construction. Suspended within this and many tensions lies a dialogical writing classroom.

Up to this point in the book, I have laid out the bare bones of a dialogical classroom and discussed ways to address the concerns that many teachers express about such practice. In Chapters 4 and 5, I will highlight specific ways that teachers enact activities and sustain projects that support dialogical writing. However, without this chapter, what I have done before and intend to do next will be mostly meaningless, for this chapter is about constructing the kind of belief system that enables teachers to take a dialogical stance on writing. Without a well-informed belief system about what constitutes a dialogical practice, individual activities have little worth.

Good teaching is like good cooking, neither of which is about following recipes. To learn to cook, to truly learn how to change unrefined food into remarkable and edifying experiences, is to learn approach and technique. The former has to do with developing a stance on what role we believe food plays in our lives and how to best engage that role. Is food about indulgence, or should we pay mind to health, or both? What happens to our cooking when we shun processed and industrialized products for local and organic ingredients? How can we create satisfying and inventive meals while also trying to limit costs? How do my culture and heritage speak to the way I conceive the role of food in my life? In our approach, we develop an evolving belief system about the preparation of food and how it all intersects with our lives.

The latter point, technique, involves understanding in broad and generic ways what occurs when we cook. What makes stir-frying different from sautéing, and when is it better to do one rather than the other? What is the purpose of egg in a recipe and, having no egg handy, what might I use in its place? If I want to generate heat and interest in a dish, what are my spice options for doing so? Through technique, we provide a framework of processes that, although miles-separated from our recipe books, allows us to cook with confidence, expediency, and creativity.

Approach and technique work the same way in the classroom. Through approach, you try to negotiate an ongoing conversation between what you believe and how you bring that belief to life in your teaching. What is your stance on how humans learn? Where do you see politics, context, sociocultural factors, genetics, and cognition playing out in the educational scheme and to what degree? How do you construct the connections and input of parents, policymakers, administration, the business community, the military, and other stakeholders within the space traditionally inhabited by teachers and students? Coming to an evolving understanding of such factors enables you to make informed decisions about the direction of your teaching.

As teachers, we always need to answer the question *why* as applied to our technique. For a given lesson, why might small groups typing responses on wiki pages be more effective than small groups marking thoughts on flip chart paper? Why should I take the time to have students write first before oral discussion on this question at this point in the lesson, but not on that question at that point? Why would a wide range of writing options for this project make more sense than the limited options I offered in the previous project? From my complex understanding of my approach and belief system—my theories of teaching and learning, if you will—I am better able to both ask and justify these questions.

In this chapter, then, I introduce you to a dozen caring and compassionate teachers who are, to my way of thinking, both remarkable and unremarkable. They are remarkable in that, when asked to share their approaches and beliefs about teaching in literacy classrooms, they were all able to do so with readiness and eloquence. Clearly, these are teachers who have reflected and continue to reflect on their practices in rich and complex ways. But it's that same quality and action that, for me, makes them unremarkable. Really, shouldn't all teachers not only be able to reflect, but also remain deeply engaged in the process of calling their practices into question?

In introducing you to these twelve teachers—all involved in the Red Clay Writing Project and/or graduate studies at the University of Georgia—I will also introduce you to qualities that I believe enhance teachers' efforts to enact dialogical stances. However, I want to caution here that there is no magical combination, nor are these the only characteristics of a strong dialogical practitioner. No one mix of qualities necessarily works for all contexts, nor do I even come close to naming and describing all the characteristics that might support such work.

Still, in this subset of teachers culled from the many doing dialogical teaching in the United States, I saw certain characteristics prevalent among them. These qualities—*seeing learning as generative, valuing relationships, evolving a learning community, combining engagement and rigor, and taking a critical stance on learning*—go far to help teachers support and sustain dialogue. My belief is that if you find yourself

Some Qualities of a Dialogical Teacher

- Seeing learning as generative
- Valuing relationships
- Evolving a learning community
- Combining engagement and rigor
- Taking a critical stance on learning

gravitating toward these qualities, then you are already well on your way toward developing the dialogical aspects of your practice.

Some Qualities of Dialogical Teachers

Who we are as teachers is bundled up tightly with who we are as people. To be sure, they are not one and the same, but one shapes the other and, to an extent, one becomes the other. Few people who see me teach imagine that I'm a basically shy and quiet man. I have learned to project a larger and more vivid persona when negotiating classrooms. That projection of myself is something I have built over time and that identity remains in process still. Yet even as that more animated identity engages in classroom dialogue, it touches base with my more socially reticent identity and establishes a healthy tension that allows for personal exploration while also staying within bounds that feel somewhat, if not completely, comfortable. For me, who we are is really better expressed as who we are becoming.

The upshot is that humans are capable of adding new facets to their burgeoning identities, but those new facets remain in dialogue with facets that are already established. One doesn't supplant the other; rather, each tugs on and shapes the other. Psychologists Hubert Hermans and Harry Kempen (1993) liken our ongoing construction of identity to that of modern composers who, by building on traditions of the past and opening themselves to a diverse range of contemporary influences, create new and complex musical forms. In these new forms, astute listeners can hear the dialogue with the established, even as that dialogue opens fresh possibilities. The music honors the past as it informs a future stance.

So it is with how we see ourselves as teachers. Our current sense of our identity is just that—a momentary understanding and not a figure carved from granite. That moment remains in dialogue with our past experience but allows us to imagine other conceptions of self. If I struggle in the moment to grasp that learning is generative, I am not destined to forever remain distant from that stance. Or if I already lean toward the belief that classrooms can be simultaneously engaging and rigorous, are there ways I might deepen that dialogue?

Just as classrooms are not static, who we are in those classrooms is also dynamic. Therefore, as I introduce these teachers and discuss how they embody some significant characteristics of a dialogical teacher, think about where you might stand in relationship to that quality. Is it one you already embrace in large ways? Something you aspire to? An aspect you don't see the need in cultivating? As with the principles discussed in Chapter 2, these characteristics are not discrete. Also, each of these teachers, although maybe stressing one characteristic more than another at any given time, remains in continuous dialogue with all of these qualities.

Seeing Learning as Generative: Ian Altman and Russ Turpin

> I always try to create an atmosphere of critical curiosity and striving for something
> more, something closer to the always approximate, indefinable truth. I encourage
> open-ended questions, and I do not encourage artificial closure (which is to say that
> I deny the reality of *all* closure). I try to do this by example. Sometimes the simple
> admission, "I don't know; I need to think on that more," as a transition from one issue
> to the next in class, can carry a great deal of weight, assuming you have students' trust
> and respect.

Can you tell that Ian Altman, the writer of this statement, studied philosophy as an
undergraduate? I now know several former philosophy students who have found
their way into education. All of them bring the same level of reflective introspec-
tion to their classroom practices. Each also deeply believes that we are makers of
meaning, that meaning is not something to be found as one might look for bugs
under rocks. Instead, meaning is something to be forged; it is, as Ian notes, "a striv-
ing for something more."

Paulo Freire (1970) captured this idea well when he described humans as
"beings in the process of becoming" (p. 72), and it is through our awareness of our
incompleteness that we seek to name the world. Doing so is "an act of creation and
re-creation" (p. 77) that is not possible unless it is infused with a love of human-
ity. For Freire, to be human is to continuously reflect and act upon that reflection,
to use word and work to develop anew our transient understandings of the worlds
around us.

From this perspective, teaching and learning are generative acts. We learn,
and I would argue that we teach, to remain in dialogue with the world around us.
As I am writing this sentence, I am both consciously and tacitly aware of the two
that preceded it. To continue my discussion, I need to, on some level, ask what I
meant by what I wrote and where those thoughts might be pointing me. What is
it that I am now coming to understand at least differently, if not better or more
deeply, because I wrote those words? Learning, when seen this way, is an active,
ongoing process that exists in the present, even as it resonates with the past and
contemplates the future.

Therefore, a writing classroom based on dialogue is one that is immersed in
text and that encourages multiple and ongoing responses to those texts. As Ian, who
teaches high school in a multicultural urban setting in northeast Georgia, put it,

> Writing constitutes the articulation of thought, even if it is not actually put onto
> paper, and so the development of skill, subtlety, imagination, and foresight in writing
> is not parallel to, but exactly the same as, the delineating of an individual's rational
> worldview. We think in language.

Social psychologist Lev Vygotsky (1962) argued that our ability to explain through language what we are thinking always falls short of our actual thoughts. However, this gap enables us to remain in a constant process of trying to share and make sense of our ideas.

> **I always try to create an atmosphere of critical curiosity and striving for something more.**
>
> **—Ian Altman**

In his classroom, Ian operationalizes this generative process by engaging students in dialogue that helps them to make the familiar strange. Together, they construct new perspectives. He urges students to seek wonderment out of what first may feel like confusion and incoherence. His point is that learning is about the hard work of figuring out your own sense of the way the world works and not relying upon information or understandings being funneled into your consciousness. Accordingly, Ian dismisses what has been construed as best practice—a term he categorizes as "a bizarre phrase for an imaginary pot of gold"—opting instead to view practice, like learning, as "something that can always be made better."

The idea of an active classroom, one in which students are constantly engaged in meaning making, is echoed by Russ Turpin. It is important for his students, mostly from working-class families living in a largely White rural county, to get beyond the complacency of playing the game of school.

> I believe that learning is socially constructed. Students can sit around, read quietly, and complete bookwork, but they're not learning anything useful if that's all we do in class. If they can read a text, then talk about both the text and their problems with the text with others, then we're moving toward actually learning something.

Like Ian, Russ knows that inquiry into our struggles helps us to generate more powerful understandings. Furthermore, Russ understands the need for students to make personal meaning from the texts they confront both in and out of the classroom. Building many daily lessons from personal journal responses, Russ has students share those responses and then has them tackle more complex and formal literary analysis. As he noted,

> I also like for students to move from their personal responses into literary analysis for texts. If students are already interested in a text based on their personal responses, I've found that they're more willing to examine those literary elements in texts. Then, when they begin to work those literary elements into their personal responses and journals, I think we've accomplished something great.

In Russ's classroom there is no clear boundary between the academic and the personal, but, similar to the work of Australian educator Barbara Kamler (2001), he creates ways for the academic and the personal to remain in dialogue, constantly generating new understandings.

> **If they can read a text, then talk about both the text and their problems with the text with others, then we're moving toward actually learning something.**
>
> **—Russ Turpin**

However, both Russ and Ian realize that without strong working relationships between teachers and students—what Russ describes as "the foundation for success in the classroom"—very little substantive meaning making will occur.

Valuing Relationships: Soria Colomer, Kristi Amatucci, and Dawan Coombs

I recall one White female student who was pregnant and would walk around school with a picture of her sonogram around her neck. She was a very happy and proud expecting mother. Well, one day I noticed that she was terribly off kilter and so I invited her to come chat with me after school if she needed to. She stopped by and silently placed her English journal on my desk. I opened it to the last entry and read about her miscarriage. However, I also saw that her teacher had written the following in red: "Are you sure this is the worst thing that could have happened to you?" [In the weeks] after we talked, I noticed that she no longer went to English class, so I suggested to the counselor that she place this student in a different English class given the circumstances. Unfortunately, she wasn't transferred and within a few weeks she dropped out of school.

Because Soria Colomer, the writer of this vignette, positioned herself as someone who tried to understand the points of view of the adolescents in the rural Mississippi county where she taught, this young woman was willing to stop by after school and share a moment of intimacy in her sorrow. As it turned out, Soria found herself attempting to repair a bridge left neglected by the student's English teacher. There was probably a range of circumstances that simultaneously converged and resulted in this young woman leaving school; the incident with her English teacher was only one. Still, what I would call a lack of sensitivity by that teacher probably caused whatever fraying ties that existed between him and the student to sever.

Regardless of the circumstances, the vignette shows the complexity and power of student–teacher classroom relationships. Freire (1970) argued that such relationships are built on love, humility, and faith. Love—in this case, love of the world, of the humans who populate it, and of the lives they lead—is an act of bravery, one that encourages openness within dialogue. Similarly, by taking a humble stance, we as teachers recognize the intelligence and potentiality of all with whom we engage, especially when we engage our students. As Freire wrote, at the point of intellectual encounter "there are neither utter ignoramuses nor perfect sages; there are only [humans] who are attempting, together, to learn more than they now know" (p. 79). Supported by love and humility, a dialogical relationship is one in which faith in the power of humans to "make and remake, to create and re-create" (p. 79) remains at the forefront. Such faith is not naïve—it sees and critiques the world; it expects better; it calls into question. Yet it remains steadfast in the belief that all of us can be transformed and are transformative.

Soria, as we'll also witness with Kristi Amatucci and Dawan Coombs in a short while, brings life to the idea of dialogical relationships being built on love, humility, and faith. Consider this excerpt from a discussion of her approach to teaching:

> My students taught me to be honest—as they would say—"keep it real." Also, I listened to my students. They knew class time was golden to me so if they had a "situation," we usually chatted a few minutes in the hallway before class started, during my planning period, or after school. They knew I'd listen, but they knew I was going to teach. Overall, I set high expectations for my students, but I established a caring atmosphere of support that let them know I would help them when they needed it—and I appreciated their help when I needed it!

It's clear that Soria is willing to see herself as a learner in her own classroom and to recognize the insight and wisdom that her students bring. It is just as clear that she is a teacher with high expectations who values the ongoing dialogue that occurs in her classroom. She makes a point of opening herself to the thoughts and needs of her students, even as she urges them toward deeper and more complex understanding of the content she provides.

> **I established a caring atmosphere of support that let them know I would help them when they needed it—and I appreciated their help when I needed it.**
>
> —Soria Colomer

Establishing classroom relationships via dialogue does not ensure that all will run smoothly or that every student will embrace you. As Soria wrote, "I have to be honest that I wasn't everyone's favorite—but I learned from those students who challenged my way of seeing the world." Through a dialogical relationship, Soria was able to see learners who resisted her practice not as annoyances to be removed from the classroom as quickly as possible, but as resources from whom she could gather multiple perspectives on her teaching. These relationships also enabled her to push students beyond what they thought they were capable of and to gently keep pressure on them to expect more of themselves as learners and citizens of the world.

> **I made every attempt to treat students as individuals who are worthy of my careful attention.**
>
> **—Kristi Amatucci**

In her multicultural, urban English classroom, Kristi Amatucci gave Freire's thoughts on love, humility, and faith her personal spin. Although she believes that existing social circumstances prevent teachers and high school students from achieving parity of power in the classroom, Kristi also argues that all classroom participants mutually construct knowledge in ways that allow each—students and teacher alike—to come away having learned what was most important for each of them to have learned. For Kristi, the best way to support such learning was "to create an atmosphere in which students felt comfortable asking questions—of me, of themselves, of one another." Yet, like Soria, Kristi did not create a fanciful search for false consensus, but instead "encouraged friendly but sometimes heated debate and tried to probe students to interrogate and intelligently defend their opinions." If students were to raise issues in her classroom, they needed to take the responsibility for imbuing their opinions with hard-won evidence and support. Kristi positioned herself to be accessible to both students and parents. As she remarked:

> I made every attempt to treat students as individuals who are worthy of my careful attention. I reached out to parents and caretakers as much as time would allow. I encouraged students to follow their interests, to publish outside of the classroom, to develop a confidence in themselves. I opened my life to students—sharing books and poems I loved, my own writing, my interests outside of school.

In such a classroom, the walls and time periods dissolve. For Kristi, her engagement with students did not exist only from 7:40 a.m. until 9:10 a.m., the time she might be designated to teach a certain course in a certain period of the day. Instead, in her attempt to "treat students as individuals who are worthy of [her] careful attention," Kristi found ways to engage with students across the day and outside the confines of her whiteboards. By seeking ways to connect with students beyond the classroom, she was better able to dialogue with them while within that space of learning.

Somewhat farther west of the Mississippi than either Soria or Kristi, Dawan Coombs taught in a high school classroom in a large city in Utah. Inspired by a quote she attributes to educational philosopher John Dewey—"What the best and wisest parent wants for his own child, that must the community want for all of its children"—Dawan sought to level a slanted playing field. It upset her that resources for education seemed to flow more readily to the schools in town that serviced families that were more affluent than those of the students who attended her school. In response to what she characterizes as an injustice, Dawan sought to create a classroom in which "all my students were served equally, with respect, and where they could take advantage of the opportunities education affords."

> I tried to be kind and caring, but I was also honest about behavior issues.
> —Dawan Coombs

Sounding almost as if she copied her response from Kristi, Dawan "tried to create a classroom environment in which students felt comfortable talking about ideas, questioning me, questioning the material, and questioning their own beliefs. I didn't want to indoctrinate them, but I did want them to read critically." To manifest that comfort with the discomfort of critique, Dawan valued relationships in class that helped students know "they were more than a grade next to a name." Like Soria and Kristi before her, Dawan saw classroom relations as complex and many-sided:

> I was super honest with them, and they were super honest with me. I tried to be kind and caring, but I was also honest about behavior issues and didn't beat around the bush when things needed to be discussed. In turn, they called me out when they thought things were unfair, when they had a question about how or why or what if, whether it pertained to the content, the school culture, or the issues we read about. I hope, above all, they knew I cared for them and that was why I did these things.

In establishing a dialogical relationship, Dawan expected students to take responsibility for themselves and their learning, even as she knew that they needed her support and encouragement. Love, tough and otherwise, was on display in her practice.

Accepting Freire at his word that love, humility, and faith go into the creation of individual classroom relationships, then what are the implications for establishing and sustaining a learning community? In particular, is establishing strong individual relationships enough to ensure a collected community dedicated to learning?

Evolving a Learning Community: Sarah Skinner, Emily Pendergrass, and Lisa Hall

> I want my classroom to be a place where we—teacher and students alike—can venture into new avenues of thinking, where there are MANY "right" answers, where we all can grow, where we are a part of something greater than ourselves as individuals—I really want to create a community, at least, and a family-feel, at best. I want all people

in my room to feel valued and appreciated. I want us all to "work hard and play hard" and to feel really accomplished and proud of ourselves when we reach the end of our time together—each day, each semester, each year.

Sarah Skinner taught and was English department chair in a large, comprehensive high school in what was, before the recession, one of the fastest sprawling suburbs of the United States. Teens who attend a school at which the student population averages more than 3,000 can easily become lost in the shuffle of so many bodies roaming through long corridors. Evolving a learning community seems one positive way to work against the anonymity and sterility of such a setting. Of necessity, such a feeling of collectivity starts with individuals being valued; however, as Sarah notes, it was important for her and her students to be "part of something greater than ourselves as individuals."

Ecological activist Derrick Jensen (2004) tells of speaking at a writers' conference held in a junior high school. As he set about getting ready for his session, he noticed a bright red bumper sticker stuck to the front of the teacher's desk where all the class could easily see it: "This is not Burger King, and you can't have it your way." Nearby was a handwritten sign in all caps: "STUDENTS MUST NEVER SPEAK WITHOUT RAISING THEIR HANDS AND BEING GIVEN PERMISSION BY THE TEACHER." If you contrast the signs in this classroom to the messages being sent by Sarah Skinner's practice, you can immediately sense in which context students were more likely to feel invited, respected, and part of a community that had their best interests at heart. Jensen, prompted by these off-putting signs, remembered his own strict schooling and sighed, "I don't know how I survived it. I don't know how any children survive it. I guess the truth is that in a very real sense many don't. And *that* is the point" (p. 197, italics in the original).

As the works of Ted Sizer (1984/2004), John Goodlad (1984/2004), Jeannie Oakes (1985/2005), Jean Anyon (1997), and others deftly illustrate, high school can be a stratifying, alienating institution. Housing upwards of 4,000 adolescents in one space has never seemed like a good idea to me. Placing them in rigid learning tracks that supposedly reflect a student's learning ability seems even less so. Shuffling learners on individual rosters from one teacher to the next creates little sense of cohesion. Even block rosters that create opportunities to work within longer class sessions largely counteract any community-building benefit by completely reshuffling the course schedule each semester.

In many ways, when children are most in need of continuity and connection—as they try to create a sense of who they are both within and outside the thrall of their families—we subject them to a maze of corridors, personalities, and subject matter, all of which feels randomly assembled and, to many of them, sadly irrelevant. Students who, through sociocultural factors such as race, ethnicity, sexual identity, or religion, find themselves on the fringes of the mainstream in their schools, may have even greater desire to feel part of a group that accepts them as they are and not as the group would have them be. Yet we tend to find institutional means to cordon off those whose only crime is difference.

> **I want my classroom to be a place . . . where we are a part of something greater than ourselves as individuals.**
>
> **—Sarah Skinner**

To run counter to this alienation and stratification, Sarah, when she teaches, tries to build community by modeling it.

> For example, when we have writing workshop time, I'm a participant. The students write; I write. The students share their writing; I share mine. I give the students feedback on their writing; they give me feedback on mine. It doesn't completely squash the hierarchy of teacher/student, but it does show them that I'm willing to be a learner alongside them. I'm also never afraid to admit that I don't know something, or that I might need to do more reading/research on my own—I showcase lifelong learning in the hopes that they, too, will embrace such a stance.

In Sarah's classroom, the line between learner and teacher becomes blurred; the classroom becomes a place where all learn and teach. In doing so, participants seek out connections that help them to relate to the ever-changing worlds they inhabit. As Sarah explained:

> I believe that all learning in school is just a part of the larger process of learning for life—everything is interconnected, and everything matters—it's just a challenge to help kids find the connections and to find the meaning in some things—that's the teacher's job: to help build those connections and inspire students to seek meaning.

Significantly, Sarah indicated that her job is to "inspire students to seek meaning" rather than provide students with meaning. The type of learning community that Sarah prefers is one in which multiple understandings prevail and learners, though supported, are expected to do the heavy lifting of coming to sense through examination, critique, dialogue, and reflection. Being part of that community requires personal passion and investment.

Emily Pendergrass teaches middle school in a once rural and mostly working-poor county that is now rapidly becoming more suburban and attracting families of wealth. She believes in letting students have increasing say in the classroom community. If students are learning together, she feels they should have more choice in defining that work. As she writes about her practice, it is not strange to hear her ask:

How long do you think this work will take? When would you like your books to be due? Do you have time tonight for homework or should we finish tomorrow? Where are you in regards to whatever we are studying? How can I help you meet your goals?

In negotiating such decisions with the group, Emily is tacitly helping her students take responsibility for their own learning. She is also getting them to better understand the connections and conflicts between individual and community needs. Nor is learning together merely about content; it also reflects deeper understandings of the social dynamics of groups.

> **A welcoming environment where the whole child is accepted and loved by me seems to take me further than anything [I've tried] before.**
> **—Emily Pendergrass**

One result of this community involvement in making decisions is that Emily believes it translates into a willingness by her students to go beyond playing the school game, of complying enough to merely get by. Having the power to change things seems to matter. Voluntarily teaching students who often struggle to succeed in other classes, Emily helps them feel included and part of a functioning unit.

> A welcoming environment where the whole child is accepted and loved by me seems to take me further than anything [I've tried] before, and I don't have battles over work. They all write poems, they all write research papers, they are all still reading lots of books and completing projects. They ALL do everything that is assigned.

Frequently teachers worry that in doing more to create community in the classroom, somehow—perhaps because students feel too welcomed or comfortable—work will slack off and school will be all about the social and not the academic. This doesn't seem to be the case, at least not in Emily's classroom. Instead, her classroom illustrates how the social and the academic must remain in dialogue.

Although not as experienced as Sarah or Emily, Lisa Hall also experiments with building community in her classroom. Using dialogue journals and other approaches that generate discussion and meaning making among her middle school students, Lisa stresses the need for students to make connections outside of themselves.

> For me, [my learning is] about the connection I make. I find it valuable to link up my life experiences to what I'm teaching, learning, or thinking about. If I can connect an idea with a movie theme or past experience, it gives the idea relevance for me. My kids don't learn exactly as I learn, but it's important to me to find their connections. I believe I have to build a reason for them to care about what I say to them as I'm talking about what I'm teaching.

In helping students develop a sense of connection to their learning, Lisa also fosters a sense of connection to one another. Lines drawn from self to text frequently get extended to peers also.

> **My kids don't learn exactly as I learn, but it's important to me to find their connections.**
>
> —Lisa Hall

Again, creation of community does not mean that all goes smoothly; it does, however, give teachers clearer insight into the bumps encountered along the way.

> Most of my students want to be treated like young adults when we discuss, but they want the freedom to be 13 when it suits them. I need to remember not to take that 13-year-old mentality too personally. In general though, I really like that my students don't mind me sitting at the lunch table with them, even though I'm a teacher. Although I don't understand why some of my students refuse to work in their assigned class periods but continue to visit my class throughout the day, I like that too. Sometimes I get discouraged and start thinking that I'm not accomplishing anything. I do have to remind myself that I'm new to teaching, and it's unrealistic to expect to have it all figured out after four years.

This last point expressed by Lisa, the sense of self-doubt, is common among what I liken to be "hungry" teachers. In moderation, I don't see doubt as a problem. Instead, it harkens to Freire's thoughts on humility; it suggests that we need to keep seeing our classes as spaces where good things occur, but perfection is still a long way down the road.

Combining Engagement and Rigor: Amy Alexandra Wilson and Trevor Thomas Stewart

> I still have a strong social justice bent, and I still have a strong commitment to providing spaces in which all sorts of diversity can thrive, including sexual diversity, religious diversity, racial diversity, socioeconomic diversity, and so forth. But, ultimately, I had at the forefront of my mind to plan classes that were just plain *fun*.

The shift in thinking that Amy Wilson is describing might at first seem contradictory: How do we address serious issues of diversity and social justice and still have fun in the classroom? Somehow we, as a society, have allowed all work in general, but schoolwork in particular, to be associated with drudgery. In this excerpt from her philosophical stance on her classroom, Amy suggests that we might be able to have it both ways, that classrooms can be sites of enjoyment even as they engage complex and substantive issues. One need not squeeze the other from the room.

Noted educational philosopher John Dewey (1938), in describing traditional rote and skill-based education, asked, "How many students, for example, were rendered callous to ideas, and how many lost the impetus to learn because of the way in which learning was experienced by them? . . . How many came to associate the learning process with ennui and boredom?" (pp. 26–27). He went on to argue that the quality of the experience—to what it is connected and how it imagines future learning engagement—matters most when teachers are deciding on activities for the classroom. As he admonished, we who educate others need to "select the kind of present experiences that live fruitfully and creatively in subsequent experiences" (p. 28). If we don't imagine classrooms in which the work environment is rich with provocation and wonderment, we create conditions where, like triples into the glove of Willie Mays, learning goes to die. "What avail is it," asked Dewey, to learn to read and write, "if in the process the individual loses his own soul?" (p. 49).

Teaching her middle school students outside Salt Lake City, Amy imagined that developing quality experiences began with the premise of bringing fun, and even silliness, into the classroom. She writes with exuberance about days when "I lost complete control of the classroom because I was laughing so hard. Middle school students are a whole lot of fun." Despite her "complete loss of control," Amy's classroom stance was driven by a quote from Henry David Thoreau: "To affect the quality of the day; that is the highest of the arts." Accordingly, Amy saw herself as an artist whose canvas was the classroom and who sought through the art of instruction to evoke emotional and thoughtful response from her learners. As she wrote,

> I wanted there to be days and moments when [my students] fundamentally enjoyed what they were doing, when they could come to class and have a good time, and when that "good time" would also be instructional time that would leave them as more critical readers, writers, thinkers, and as more compassionate people.

Like Dewey, Amy believes that experience alone isn't enough; that experience needs to create joyful moments that lead not only to present and future learning, but to the love of learning as well.

But, ultimately, I had at the forefront of my mind to plan classes that were just plain *fun*.

                                                                                —Amy Alexandra Wilson

---

Perhaps the best word to describe Amy's middle school classroom would be *active*—she was an active teacher engaging active students in active exploration: persuasive essays were written to be delivered as speeches; haikus were as easily devised outdoors as in; parents and community members were always welcome to share their life experiences; English scripts were written for Bollywood movies;

class discussions often focused on what the group was to read next; community service projects were developed that required students to research the issues and write about their experiences; self-written scary stories were shared in a darkened classroom around a lantern subbing for a campfire. Fun? Certainly. Work? Most assuredly. Learning? Absolutely.

Teaching on the other side of the country in the mountains of North Carolina, Trevor Stewart "tried to keep the atmosphere in my classroom serious but fun, which is, admittedly, a tough line to walk." Like their counterparts in Utah, Trevor and his students, many of them from White or Native American working-poor families, found much to laugh about, even as they focused on the complex work of literacy classrooms.

> The serious bit was that I made no bones about the fact that I expected big things from them. Saying, "I can't" wasn't allowed. I always said, "Can't means won't. You might not know how yet, but you will." And I wasn't afraid to say that sternly. The fun bit was that I liked to joke around a lot with them. If I made a mistake, said something goofy, misspelled a word on the chalkboard, or whatever, I wasn't afraid to be the butt of a *friendly* joke. . . . That cuts both ways, though. I would give my students a hard time, too, when they said goofy things.

Before you characterize Trevor as a bully, you need to understand his relationship to his students. Even he admits that this two-way joking is "hard to describe" outside the context of his classroom, but it's much akin to the ways Mikhail Bakhtin (1986) has described the power and role of laughter in learning. It is through laughter that we discover and sustain hope. While "seriousness burdens us with hopeless situations" (p. 134), laughter allows us to rise above and liberate ourselves from such doubts. Laughter, when shared in "joyful, open" ways "only unites; it cannot divide" (p. 135). When we teach in classrooms that are devoid of laughter—when rote and lifeless writing assignments fill the minutes of our learning day—we condemn students and teachers to learning that is inert and sterile. Regarding such contexts, Bakhtin sighed parenthetically, "The dogmatist gains nothing; he cannot be enriched" (p. 142).

They have to know that you are interested in their lives, and their lives have to be a crucial part of what's going on in the classroom.

—Trevor Thomas Stewart

But achieving the "social, choral nature of laughter" (Bakhtin, 1986, p. 135) requires that teachers find many ways to get to know their students and the many facets of the lives students live beyond campus. "Relationships are key," notes Trevor, and he goes on to explain,

They have to know that you are interested in their lives, and their lives have to be a crucial part of what's going on in the classroom. . . . So I went to their baseball/softball games, coached the shooting team (we were in the middle of nowhere—schools in the middle of nowhere have shooting teams), and I talked with them in the hallways about what was going on in their lives. Then, I took that information and weaved it into our classroom discussions about literature. It's funny, if you know that Sierra and Travis (two of my students) are from totally different social groups but date anyway, it's a whole lot easier to make *Romeo & Juliet* relevant.

From the development of classroom relationships comes laughter; from the laughter comes relationships. That ongoing process leads to learning.

Both Amy and Trevor enact classrooms in which students are expected to do the hard work of learning, but also to find enjoyment and engagement in work that challenges and sustains. It's in such an atmosphere, Bakhtin (1986, p. 135) argued, that creativity and excellence reside:

Everything that is truly great must include an element of laughter. Otherwise it becomes threatening, terrible, or pompous; in any case, it is limited. Laughter lifts the barrier and clears the path.

Taking a Critical Stance: Angela Dean and Paige Cole

In the quote written by Angela Dean that opened this chapter, she explained that although she may want her classroom to be a safe space for students and that she might try hard to achieve that, safety cannot be guaranteed, nor is playing it safe always desirable. Later on, in the same piece of writing, Angela offered these thoughts:

I hope to have [my students] leave with compassion for one another, an open mind for voices and experiences that are different from their own, and a sense of agency to create change for themselves and for others.

Such is the balancing act of all who take a critical stance on teaching. How do you create forums for dialogue that enable students to ask and explore hard questions that matter to them and still enable all participants to emerge from those discussions as open and caring citizens of a diverse world?

I believe that learning is not a safe act. If it were, I don't think we'd truly be learning.

—Angela Dean

In the words of Quantz, Rogers, and Dantley (1991), "Authoritarianism creates alienation; authority creates community" (p. 102). However, the process of moving toward this kind of community makes for many volatile moments—emotionally, intellectually, culturally—in the rehearsal halls we call classrooms. If I push this rehearsal metaphor, the classroom is not a static place where knowledge is arrived at, but instead is a place of becoming, where knowledge and teaching are under construction and constant refinement. It is here that we who teach engage in a kind of organic choreography, one that eventually finds fluidity out of the fits and starts of our practice.

In that mirrored hall, we rehearse moves as means for commenting on the world in which we live, but, upon reflection, call those moves into question. In such a space, both comfort and discomfort are to be experienced in the scrutiny. As we try on new roles and perspectives, awkwardness returns; we stumble where we once were graceful. This shifting of intentions and purposes blurs and challenges lines of authority, creating new relationships in the classroom dynamic.

It is not that notions of authority are either completely assumed or completely dismissed in dialogical classrooms—quite the contrary. Such notions are negotiated and made complex. In part, Angela sets out to create a sense of wobble in all of her students, to have them consider that perspectives exist in the world that differ from the ones they and others like them hold. Noting that her school serves both an affluent upper-middle-class population and children from immigrant and/or working-class families of less wealth and political influence, Angela challenges both groups to dialogue:

> I knew that the school would have a dichotomy such as this, and I wanted to teach
> both groups. I wanted to teach those without the position of power how to find voice,
> and I wanted to teach those within the position of power how to use their voice in
> ways that helped more than just themselves.

Her classes are designed to be safe spaces; however, learning in a safe space does not equate to learning at a distance. It does not mean that cultures and experiences are packed away and, along with all emotional investment, left at the classroom door, only to be picked up, like a book bag, upon the ringing of the bell.

Angela intentionally complicated the concept of *safe space*. Instead of devising a classroom in which the students are *safe from* ideas or difficult discussions, she creates a space where it is *safe to* engage in personally challenging explorations and lines of inquiry that call thinking into question (Fecho, Collier, Friese, & Wilson, 2010).

> I wanted to challenge my students, most of whom I knew would come from affluent
> homes, to see what stake they had in power and control. I wanted them to become
> more cognizant of their positions of power simply as a result of their being born to
> middle- and upper-class families [and] living in a suburban community. I have also
> worked on the opposite end of the spectrum in our school to help promote those who

have little to no advocacy from home to feel more a part of the school community. These students are typically placed in our technical track. They come from working-class and single-parent homes. They come from immigrant parents who do not know the language of their new country, much less the one of the dominant power group and school. They come from little expectation to succeed and have bought into the expectation—offered by former teachers and administrators—that they will always be apathetic, so why bother?

When such divergence of experience and perspective meets in a classroom, it can feel uncomfortable, and even threatening, for students and teachers. Invitations to dialogue, and the acceptance of those invitations, involve risk and uncertainty for everyone. This context points at the paradox of creating a space where it is *safe to* engage, inquire, and dialogue, but, at times, such a space may feel very *un*safe.

Like many of the teachers profiled earlier, Angela is able to negotiate hard talk with her students because she has taken the time to develop classroom re-lationships with them and have them develop classroom relationships with one another. Along with actions such as using personal writing to make textual and interpersonal connections to literature and encouraging peers to support the school activities of classmates, Angela invests much energy in group collaboration.

> I believe that allowing them to work in groups can be powerful for them and for me. I can hear more from those kids who don't always offer their voice in whole-class discussions when I have them work in groups, and it is easier to gauge where they are in their understanding or reflection of a topic. I also believe that groups chal-lenge them to speak and share; they can't get out of providing their voice or sharing a piece of writing because the expectation is there that all of the group will participate. They sort of keep one another accountable. I feel that working in various groupings throughout the year helps to build a sense of community and connects kids who may not have otherwise chosen to work together. It allows them to open their minds to perspectives of people who are possibly different than themselves.

From such community comes the willingness to risk and honor diverse perspective, to shift the class from one that keeps all participants *safe from* the discomfort of self-reflection to one in which it is *safe to* work through that discomfort.

Paige Cole shows similar interest in having her students express themselves intellectually on cultural and political issues. Teaching social studies in a high school in which a rural, working-class population and a more suburban-oriented middle class mingle in the same corridors, Paige starts lessons with what her stu-dents bring with them.

> I care about what my students think and what they think about, which can be an emo-tionally charged place to be; however, I would not know how to work any other way. The kind of dialogue that we engage in within my classroom, with all of the voices

and past histories coming into play, creates a space that feels alive to me and changes me—as much, if not more—than it changes any of my students.

Although acknowledging the charged emotionality of a classroom in which multiple perspectives are encouraged, she is adamant that it's the only way to catch lightning in a classroom.

Moreover, as has been mentioned time and again by the teachers profiled here, authentic dialogue occurs only when teachers immerse themselves in the critical processes of learning along with their students. This engagement cannot be a sham performance. As Paige acknowledges, "I have come to believe that one of the most wonderful and frustrating things about working with teenagers is their ability to detect when you are faking it." Instead, she attempts to offer her open and candid perspective on classroom issues, even when topics such as the struggle for civil rights in the United States or the attempted annihilation of European Jews by Nazism exposes the unseemly underbelly of humankind. "I try to tell the truth," writes Paige, "but also realize that my truth may not be the same as my students'."

> **I care about what my students think and what they think about, which can be an emotionally charged place to be.**
>
> —Paige Cole

A bottom line for Paige is that students need to seek and constantly refine the meanings they derive from engagement with the world around them.

I hope I am teaching my students to think in a critical manner without breeding cynicism or disconnecting them from the beliefs that sustain them. I want them to have the space to work on their own ideas, and I want myself to have the patience to support this sometimes elusive objective. For me, teaching social studies is not about dates and names, but about first trying to understand who we are today before we begin communing with the past.

Similar to Angela, Paige understands and places into practice the notion that learning is an active process of calling our world into question and then generating a more nuanced understanding of that world in the process.

Putting It All Together

The sharp reader might gather by now that each teacher profiled in this section, to some extent, embraces all five of the qualities discussed herein. Paige does not just bring a critical stance to her work but also sees learning as a generative act, values classroom relationships, supports community, and fosters engagement and rigor. The same could be said for the other eleven.

Questions You Might Ask Yourself

- What qualities of a dialogical teacher already seem to be among my strengths?

- What might I learn from the teachers described here?

- What aspect of my teaching do I most want to focus on in order to support dialogical practice?

- If I were to write my philosophical stance on teaching, what would I include?

Similarly, these teachers don't display or work on these qualities individually but, instead, represent them in practice in ways that promote continual dialogue. A given class might be pitched more toward, say, constructing community, but all the other qualities will find their way to the surface and resonate with the current focus. And, as mentioned earlier, other qualities, such as recognizing the importance of culture and organizing learning through frameworks, simultaneously become part of the conversation. To enter a dialogical classroom is to enter a crowded space. Much is being thought, said, and offered there.

Having started this chapter with her voice, I think it only appropriate to end with this vignette from Angela. As she relates the story of her experience working with one Latino student, we see Angela weaving the qualities described in this chapter through her practice. As you read, think about the way her approach and technique talk to each other. Read the vignette again and consider what a remarkable teacher she is. Then think about what remarkable company she shares in this chapter. Finally, remember that you, too, are remarkable.

I'd like to think that I cultivate a warm and supportive relationship with my students. I know that this isn't always true and that there are kids who just won't let you in or who are not ready to trust you even after a year's worth of work together. I feel that I do reach more than I haven't.

I have one student who was on the verge of dropping out when I first met him. He is from Los Angeles and his parents are immigrants from Mexico. He is estranged from his biological father, but his mom has remarried. He was a 17-year-old sophomore when I first met him. He kept to himself and his head was often down in class. He actually did leave school for a few months and was officially withdrawn, but returned to Georgia and to our school the following semester.

On his return, I didn't press him about where he'd been, but instead welcomed him and worked to make him feel a part of our classroom community. I nominated him for our Spring Honors night; since his return he had maintained an A or B in our class. Again, at the end of the semester, he considered dropping out. He met with his guidance counselor who felt he had a better chance with a GED than a diploma, talked to his parents, and felt he'd made the decision to go.

He came to see me on what he thought would be his last day. I told him that I didn't judge him for his decision, that he knew what was best for him. I did encourage him to at least finish the semester, but reminded him that the choice was his to make.

He decided to stay and is now looking to start his last year of school.

Exploring Dialogical Writing Projects

T he physical space of Kristi Amatucci's classroom at Piney Creek High
School—all school names in this book are pseudonyms—was typical of classrooms at other schools built within recent years: a little
smaller than it should be and crowded with desks so that cohorts of
up to thirty adolescents could share time there throughout the day. It's difficult
in such spaces to blunt the impact of that much furniture massed within concrete blocks broken by few windows. Still, Kristi managed to soften the textures
with plants on the windowsills, decorations on the walls, books for lending,
and four floor lamps arranged in the room's corners. That last touch—torchères
that let light spill out over the top of the shade and play off the walls and ceil-
ings—allowed Kristi to turn off the harsh fluorescents overhead. During writing
or group times, the warm light glowed with the feel of an old-world library.
With the lighting hushed, the din of the classroom followed suit.

Piney Creek is located in a small city in the southeastern United States that
is dominated by a large university. Although the White population in the county
hovers around 65 percent, that same population represents only 20 percent of

the students in the district. Working-class and working-poor Blacks and Latinos are the county's prime consumers of public education. To position against the stereotype of neglect of public education when White flight occurs, the school district has made an infrastructure investment in education, with all schools in the district either being built anew or going through the process of comprehensive upgrades.

It was in this context that Kristi, now an aspiring teacher educator, would ask her students to make meaning of their own experiences. As is often done in dialogical projects, Kristi's plan started with the lives of her students, getting them to write in small and intimate ways about commonplace events. Working from prompts provided by her—for example, a time when students argued with a friend; a lesson they learned from a family member; a situation in which they changed their mind about someone/something—students would use these reflections to call attention to details in their day-to-day lives with hope of seeing underlying significance.

The students also wrote with the intention of connecting to ongoing discussions of literature. At the same time, Kristi had class members read personal narratives by published authors. Pieces by the likes of Malcolm X, Sandra Cisneros, Elie Wiesel, Maxine Hong Kingston, and Charlayne Hunter-Gault provided her high school writers not only with insight into the lives of provocative people, but also visions of the craft of writing personal narrative. Typically, the class would read a short piece and respond in writing on the same day. They'd do two or three of these literature responses per week for a couple of weeks. Kristi also had students search out personal narratives, primarily those found in two sections of *Newsweek* magazine—"My Turn" and "The Last Word"—to which the class had a subscription.

I'm going to let Kristi's voice pick up the explanation at this point:

I collected all of these written reflections and read them. Instead of "grading" each reflection, I wrote comments in response and returned them to students as soon as possible. Some of the reflections were also shared with classmates and, in some cases, with the class as a whole. After reading a variety of personal narratives and writing several informal reflections on personal experiences, students were asked to select one of the reflections and turn it into a polished personal narrative of three to five typewritten pages.

As students wrote these narrative pieces, they shared them with classmates and with persons outside of class who might help them remember details of the experience. I also read and commented on drafts. Sometimes this commentary took the form of oral conferences rather than written comments. On the date the final narratives were due, students were invited to share them with classmates, although if a student preferred not to share, I didn't force the issue.

With her high school ascribing to the six-trait writing rubric (for a full description, see Blasingame & Bushman, 2005), Kristi would then grade the narratives. However, students were also encouraged to self-assess, both through use of the same rubric and by inclusion in a reflective end-of-semester portfolio.

In considering the impact of this work, Kristi told of how this project was well received and executed by her students. In particular, she indicated that the opportunity for students to bring their lives into the classroom and her valuing of such writing was one factor that helped gel her somewhat random collection of learners into a more cohesive learning community. As she explained:

> After reading an excerpt from *The Autobiography of Malcolm X* that our textbook editors entitled "Hair," the class engaged in a spirited, hour-long discussion about hair and body modifications they had either experimented with or were curious about. Sophisticated questions were posed and conflicting arguments aired: What can we make of the multibillion dollar industry in hair products? What motivates some individuals and not others to become obsessed with inking their bodies? Should wait staff in a local restaurant be required to remove nose rings when on the job? Why are teenagers encouraged by parents when they choose to dye their hair blond but questioned when they choose to dye it blue? In contrast with more orchestrated class discussions, almost every student participated in this one, and it continued for the remainder of the period.
>
> Following the lively discussion, several students wrote narratives in response to topics that were raised by the class. Katherine wrote about her parents' reaction to her older sister's decision to get a tattoo. Charlissa's narrative, like Malcolm X's, focused on the memory of her first perm, which came at age seven. Nick wrote the story of how he was marginalized within his church youth group after he pierced his ear. Students wrote pieces that were longer than the required number of words and better in quality than others they wrote during the same semester.

The multiple transactions with text enabled students not only to value their varied experiences, but also to understand how the experiences of others shaped, and could continue to shape, their lives.

Framing the Dialogical Writing Project

I'll refer again to the idea that, like Kristi herself, what she created for her classroom is both remarkable and unremarkable. Given the micromanagement by administration of so many middle and high school classrooms, it is remarkable that a project so connected and integrated could be carried out. That point noted, it's a personal narrative writing project; it asks students to write about themselves in thoughtful ways. To that extent, it's fairly commonplace and eminently doable.

supporting to work student in dialogical way

dialogical writing

That's not a knock on Kristi's project; I think it's great. That's one reason it's leading off the chapter. However, I do want to stress that Kristi is neither more nor less creative than any other teacher. It's not the project itself that makes the activity remarkable; it's how she supported the work in dialogical ways that matters.

Recall the discussion in Chapter 1 in which I suggested that dialogical writing is built on the following framework. Such writing . . .

- represents an intersection of academic and personal writing;
- allows writers to bring multiple voices to the work;
- involves thought, reflection, and engagement across time and located in space; and
- creates opportunities for substantive and ongoing meaning making.

Take a moment to read back through the description of Kristi's project, using this framework as a lens. Consider how the components of her project build outwardly from this frame, giving it flesh and depth and substance. Go. Give it a read. Don't worry about me. I'll be here when you get back.

In Kristi's classroom, students were dialoguing—authoring responses—in multiple ways to multiple texts. They read published narratives and reacted to them. They read their self-written narrative starts and also responded. In doing both, they called their own insights into question as they did for that of others. Furthermore, Kristi dialogued with her students, obviously during class discussion, but also by responding to this low-stakes writing as a reader and not as an evaluator. Even family members and friends were invited into the dialogical transaction. Many voices were brought to all texts with the hope of gaining many perspectives.

Text was seen as substantive—we can learn from what is in print before us—but also malleable—we can call it into question and render it in new ways. An activity that is literature-based was linked to a writing-based activity, and both were then extended into a more formal project. Kristi immersed her students in reading, writing, listening, and speaking activities that were all predicated on helping them make new understandings for themselves. By prolonging the dialogue through multiple responses, Kristi enabled reflection and meaning making to occur across time and to build on itself. Events of the past were crystallized in the present with the intent of framing future exploration.

Through this activity, students transacted with formal structures—they used published narratives as mentor texts—while reflecting on the needs, concerns, and victories great and small of the lives they led. Because the stories they generated sprang from a range of sources and were responded to in

Dialogical Writing in Kristi's Project

- Short, spontaneous pieces written as responses to literature
- Brief reflections that plumbed life events of the students
- Extended narratives springing from the shorter reflections

multiple ways, the students were doing what Kamler (2001) has called relocating the personal. As she noted, "What the writer produces is a text, a story, that comes from her, but is *not* her" (p. 177, italics in the original). Simultaneously, the writing retains the personal story of the writer as it makes use of the necessary distance and structures of more formal genres. In doing so, students learn how to craft writing without losing themselves in the process.

As you read through the rest of this chapter, routinely return to this framework and consider how each teacher embraces those components and brings them to life in a range of ways. Think about how this structure allows for limitless variations on a theme. Certainly, by the end of this chapter and the next, you have the potential, at least, to add a dozen proven dialogical writing projects to your list of effective classroom activities. However, my hope, and I think that of the teachers represented here, is that by dialoguing with these twelve examples, you'll feel much more confident about improvising your own spins off the frame. By realizing that the framework offers multiple opportunities for variation and by taking the dialogical stance suggested in the previous chapter, you become the author of multiple responses to the pedagogy suggested here and your own vital practice. Rather than a collector, we prefer you become a generator of dialogical writing projects.

Crafting Dialogical Writing Projects from the Framework

In the remainder of the chapter and through all of the next, I take you inside eleven classrooms—some urban, some suburban, some rural, some in transition—strewn across the South and West of the United States. Within each classroom, the students and teachers are engaged in ongoing dialogue—with one another, with themselves, and with a range of texts. Every teacher described here is capable of days that feel like magic in their seamlessness and productivity, but all also have days when the ending bell doesn't come fast enough. What I describe here is practice that, in the context given, seemed to play out in ways that were useful and dynamic for teachers and students alike.

Glimpses into classrooms are always tricky. They are snapshots, frozen moments. They both inform and distort our understanding of that classroom. To help mitigate this concern a bit, I've added some description of school and classroom contexts to the teaching philosophies discussed in Chapter 3. Regardless, we will only know a soupçon of how community was created and how relationships grew from the transactions of teachers and students. My hope is that a little will be enough to help you grasp the complexity and possibility of each of these learning spaces.

Largely as a matter of convenience, I've arranged this series of classroom visits using the relative time frames for project completion as an organizer. In other words, projects taking less classroom time have been arranged first, followed by mid-range projects. In Chapter 5, the focus will be extended projects, and particular emphasis will be placed on seeing these dialogical writing projects as examples of what Grant Wiggins (1998) has called educative assessment. Regardless of the length of time required to complete the projects, what each shares with the others is a dedication to have all classroom participants engage in dialogue. It is in this dialogue, one that requires them to interrogate their burgeoning perspectives even as they call into question the worlds they are coming to explore, that meaning is made.

Short-Range Projects: Soria Colomer, Ian Altman, and Trevor Stewart

Before starting her doctoral studies, Soria Colomer taught Spanish at Silver Lake, a high school in a town of the same name in Mississippi. When she taught there, Soria was the only Latina/Latino on a faculty that was roughly two-thirds Black and one-third White. Of the 500 to 600 students who matriculate at the school in any given year, more than 80 percent are Black, with Whites and a handful of Latinos making up the remainder. Much of the White population of the region, at least those who can afford to do so, send their children to a private academy. The result is that Silver Lake is a school that has become, as Soria noted, "divided by race but united by class."

The building itself reflects a kind of school architecture that is reminiscent of European castles and college campuses like Cambridge. Nothing so grand, but the façade of arched doorways, parapets, and scrollwork was meant for the school to be seen, no doubt, as a fortress of learning. Unlike Kristi's school described at the start of the chapter, Silver Lake had been built with a sense of largesse, and the rooms, although perhaps needing renovation, were spacious and easily accommodated groups of thirty.

Given the complicated race and class structure that surrounded her, Soria felt it very necessary to engage students across borders of race and ethnicity to encourage widening of perspectives. In particular, she worried that stereotypical images of Latinos would continue to dominate how many Blacks and Whites perceived students who came from families in which the first language was Spanish. Being of Honduran heritage, Soria knew well how people in the United States often conflate all Latinos with Mexicans, completely disregarding differences in culture between Latin American countries. She had also experienced firsthand a lack of tolerance for anyone speaking Spanglish, a creative and frequently necessary blending of Spanish and English.

With these issues in mind, Soria constructed a project for students in her Spanish classes to begin the dialogue that could lead to more nuanced understandings of the diverse nature of the growing Latino population in the United States.

She also hoped students would gain some insight into the ways our language and identities under construction shape each other. As you read through the summary of the activity, think about how Soria framed the work so it would be a dialogue and not some prearranged perspective she wanted her students to grasp. What she does particularly well is create opportunities for substantive and ongoing meaning making through thought and reflection, all within a relatively short time frame.

Designed to fit into claustrophobic fifty-minute periods of which Soria taught six in a day, this simple two-day activity began with the playing of an MP3, "Shorty, Shorty," a classic boy-chases-girl love song sung in Spanglish by Xtreme. She asked her students to react to what they heard and to also describe the group they envisioned performing the song. Soria followed with the video that illustrates the music and then had students unpack how their images contrasted with how the group actually appears. As a way of pulling the dialogue together, she had her students read and analyze the lyrics with an eye and ear toward what cues allowed them to understand the Spanish–English mix.

> **Dialogical Writing in Soria's Project**
>
> - Written reactions to music and videos
> - Group charting of lyric analysis and code-switching implications
> - Monologue based on unpacking of language issues and stereotypes

A second day of exploration began with another video— "Cuando Volveras" by Aventura—followed by a discussion about who the students thought listened to such music and how the videos did or didn't challenge their views of Latinos. In particular, the focus for this session was on language as Soria broke her class into groups to discuss their motivations for code-switching in their own lives and how such blending of codes related to Spanglish. "Who," she asked, "might appreciate the blending of language in this video and who, perhaps, wouldn't?" Selecting a character type from that student-generated list (e.g., immigrant student, second-generation student, math teacher, parent, White farmer, state legislator, etc.), students wrote a monologue that had their character discussing language use in general and the complexities of code-switching in particular. In this paper that was completed at home, students were encouraged to avoid stereotypes and instead present their character's issues in a balanced way.

Ian Altman also saw connections between perceptions and the worlds of performance and art. From his classroom at Torrance Central, the other comprehensive high school located in the same city in which Kristi taught, Ian asked his students to consider the connections that might exist between literature, writing, and other fine arts. Most important, he was seeking to have his students react not just analytically to art and performance, but emotionally as well—what Rosenblatt (1995) has called efferent and aesthetic response respectively. As he envisioned this dialogical project, he was intent on having students work from personal response toward deeper analytic appreciation. Students would be dialoguing with literature, art, and music in ways that asked them to bring an emotional response before they pushed toward a more nuanced sense of meaning.

About three times larger in student population than Silver Lake, Torrance Central still manages to replicate the school-as-fortress-of-learning motif, but in ways more abstract and linear than its Mississippi counterpart. Also, as the school has grown, glass-walled and peaked-roof additions have created a sense of suburban sprawl grafted to the more institutional main building. Blacks make up slightly more than half of the student body, with Whites roughly a quarter, and Latinos and a smaller Asian population completing the graph. Running four ninety-minute classes a day on semester rotation, the school is also divided into college preparatory, advanced college preparatory, gifted, and advanced placement levels, although this labeling is a bit deceiving. The college preparatory track would be called regular or basic track in most high schools and, with few exceptions—Ian's class being one of them—students in that track aren't necessarily prepared for university learning.

Walking into Ian's classroom on consecutive days, you'd be likely to find the room arranged differently from the day before. As Ian explained:

> Sometimes [students] are in rows (though I try to make irregular rows to give an impression of order without militarism); sometimes they are in groups of three, four, or five, depending on what they will be doing. Sometimes I allow them to choose their own groups, and other times I choose the groups for them, usually to allow as much interpersonal comfort as possible or to facilitate differentiated tasks and instruction, again depending on what we will be doing on the given day.

Rather than have the room arrangement dictate the work that will occur there, Ian uses the work as a reason to create a room arrangement that facilitates the process.

Dialogical Writing in Ian's Classroom

- Open genre reaction to musical selection
- Students writing about issues of moral ambiguity in short story and their lives
- Open genre piece making connections across music, story, and painting
- Group or individual development of pieces started in class

Ian test-flew this project with a class of ninth-grade advanced college preparatory (ACP) students, but has modified versions of the work for all his sections. This ACP class—predominantly equal parts Black students and White students augmented by Asian, Eastern European, and Latino immigrants—seemed open to the new and unusual, and was where Ian liked to experiment with his instruction. In particular, he noted that students in this class tended "to be good readers, if not always subtle readers," and so this project was devised to build on the former while helping to improve the latter. Because the texts—a piece of classical music, a short story by Hemingway, and a painting by Picasso—carry the weight of being encased in their respective canons, a first glance at this project might seem ponderous. But Ian has framed these works, and the dialogues around them, in ways that provide students with multiple means of access. He tried to allow opportunities for students to find themselves in the work and construct a sense of relevance to it.

After explaining what he considered to be the difference between active listening and passive hearing, Ian asked his students to listen to the three short but dramatic movements of *Gaspard de la Nuit* by Ravel. Using the time allotted by ninety-minute block scheduling, Ian gave his students thirty minutes to write freely and in any genre in response to the music. Specifically, he stressed that "however the writing turns out, I want them to allow the music to affect them, to let the music seep into their deepest consciousness, and to react accordingly in writing." Student volunteers then shared part or all of what they had written, and a dialogue on the range of emotional reaction elicited by the music followed.

The next class then built on the dramatic music of Ravel by asking students to read "The Denunciation," a Hemingway tale set during the Spanish Civil War. After first delivering a mini-lecture to provide students with a historical context, Ian gave them class time to read and share initial reactions to the story. That night at home, students wrote short pieces that asked them to unpack the theme of moral ambiguity in the story and how such a theme may have played out in their lives. Ian knows that if you ask students to write on something the night before, you need to forefront that writing the day after in class. Excited by the complexity of what occurs in morally ambiguous situations, students talked at length about their own experiences and the connections they saw between their experience and the short story.

On the third day of the project, Picasso's depiction of the firebombing of Guernica moved front and center. Ian asked students "to look at it for some minutes, much like they listened to *Gaspard de la Nuit*, and again allow it to seep into their consciousness, paying attention to the lines of figurement and disfigurement, the various eyes in the painting, and the general mood set by it." And, as with the music and short story, students were invited to write in a genre that suited them, but this time to draw connections across all three artistic pieces. Given the option of working alone or in small groups, students took a few days to polish their works, and those who were willing shared them with the class.

What attracts me in this work, aside from the way it encourages students to see the personal in the formally artistic, is how Ian had no expectations, as he put it, "that anyone would have the same tastes as I have." Instead, his intent was to have students "let great art affect them sincerely in some way." Agreement as to the likeability of the piece was not a requirement:

> Some students did not at all like Ravel's music, and commented that they prefer music to have words, or a steady beat, or not to last so long, or all of the above. Some said

simply that it was boring. Comments such as these were few, though, and I expected them.

Instead, what Ian prized more was the engagement and response—that his students found some way to connect to art and to see how art connects to other works. Fully admitting that the project requires "some very deep and difficult philosophical thinking," he also recognized and expected that with "patience and care," students can navigate those straits.

When teaching at Laurel County High School in the North Carolina mountains, Trevor Stewart also sought ways to help his rural White and Native American students have greater access to literature works, particularly that of Shakespeare. Like Silver Lake, Soria's high school, Laurel County houses around 550 students, too many of whom live in poverty. This problem is exacerbated by the county's proximity to Great Smoky Mountains National Park that, on one hand, affords spectacular views from the classrooms of the school, but, on the other, makes economic development difficult because the land is under federal jurisdiction. Perhaps owing some architectural kinship to the work of Frank Lloyd Wright, Laurel County High School doesn't call attention to itself. It's a well-maintained, one-story brick ramble that tries to be of, rather than apart from, its surroundings.

As is the case in many high schools, Laurel County students are grouped by supposed ability levels, and Trevor frequently taught ninth-grade general track students. Self-admittedly, the room Trevor welcomed his students into was "by all appearances . . . a plain, boring space." He even admits to keeping his desks in straight rows ("Gasp! I know. A teacher who values dialogue teaching in rows!"). But, like all good dialogical teachers, he had his reasons. In this case, straight rows facilitated his being able to access students easily in the cramped space of his class-room. And, when useful, students could shift desks into clusters or lounge on the floor during reading time.

When students were reading a play by Shakespeare or some other compli-cated text, Trevor would trot out a dialogical activity he called "key quotes." It was one he adapted from Jim Nicholmy, a professor who had taught Trevor as an undergraduate. Somewhat like his classroom, there's nothing fancy in Trevor's project, but if the point is to get students to make personal meaning of complicated text, then it gets the job done.

For any given scene, Trevor told his students to select a quote that they felt was significant to their understanding of the tragedy.

Dialogical Writing in Trevor's Project

- Students select and explain significance of quotes from literature reading
- Thematic essay developed from their key quote pieces

As Trevor explained, "The main idea was for them to enter into some dialogue with the play as they were reading it. I wanted to get some insight into what the students were picking up on as they attempted to transact with some very difficult reading." This emphasis on students determining that which they feel is important in the text is key here. It's what shifts what could be construed as a close-ended comprehension check into a more dialogical experience. Trevor imagines his students to be meaning makers. As such, he gives them the tools and opportunities to initiate dialogue that will personally illuminate the text for each student rather than imposing some historically validated, but impossibly threadbare, interpretation of the text.

In selecting an excerpt, students needed to explain its context and then discuss why they saw it as significant. Of course, the short writings were shared in class and used to spark further dialogue about what they were all coming to understand individually and collectively. Ultimately, students were able to go back through their many key quote writings and develop a longer thematic essay. Similar to the work of Soria and Ian already discussed, Trevor's project nested shorter and lower-staked writing tasks inside a longer and higher-staked writing project. From Trevor's stance, the point to remember is that "the process . . . is the key element, and the product is just a way to help guide the way we used process."

In the examples provided by Soria, Ian, and Trevor, the dialogical projects are contained and focused. Yet even in their relative brevity, their projects carry the qualities of all writing projects that seek to be more dialogical. Each project represents an intersection of academic and personal writing: Soria's students informally reacted to music videos in which Spanglish is featured and then developed more polished responses; Ian's class used a range of genres to initially react in writing to art and then refined and expanded one of those reactions; and Trevor's learners made written meaning of self-selected text excerpts before using those discussions to develop richer essays. To make that blending occur, students dialogued on the page and in person with themselves, the teacher, the texts, and their peers. Time and opportunity were provided to help students to be engaged and reflective over time and across activities. Finally, students were made responsible for constructing meaning. Ample support was provided through the process, but, in the end, students needed to arrive at understandings based on their many written explorations.

Mid-Range Projects: Paige Cole, Emily Pendergrass, and Lisa Hall

I often remark to the preservice and inservice teachers who populate my classes that anything I suggest in terms of teaching will slow down their curriculum. It's true. I hold to the Coalition of Essential Schools belief (2010) that less is more. It's better, from my perspective, to explore substantive concepts and unearth all of

each dialogic projects involves academic and personal writing...

less is more

their rich complexity than to rush headlong through an overcrowded program of study under the delusion that, because I walked them past an idea, students have developed what Wiggins and McTighe (2005) call enduring understanding. To believe that learners will have a firm grasp on the subtleties of a literary term such as *irony* merely because I included it on a vocabulary list and quizzed for it on Friday is to be blinded by hope. Such approaches to teaching account for why irony is so often ascribed to events that are merely curious. Unless we find ways for students to reflect, to mull, to reconsider, to contemplate, to wonder, or to just plain stew, we deny them, and eventually society, the benefits that come from taking the time to construct layered and nuanced meaning.

Despite the ever-growing curriculum that surrounds her content area, social studies teacher Paige Cole is willing to slow down her instruction in an attempt to help her Yamasee High School students gain deeper understanding. Located in a once rural county populated primarily by working-class Whites, Yamasee now is witness to the sprawl of the Atlanta metro area, which is changing farmland into subdivisions and commercial building sites. The school is relatively new—actually built in response to this influx of middle-class population—and is a metal-roofed, gabled edifice that sprawls in its own way. Filtering through its four daily blocks is a student population that is 70 percent White, with Blacks, Latinos, and Hmong composing the remainder. Perhaps mirroring the class divide that presents itself at Yamasee, Paige's advanced placement classes, by her account, seem to be newcomer heavy, whereas her regular classes more often represent families long associated with the area. Currently hovering around 1,500 students, the school population is an interesting flux of cultures negotiating a common space.

Paige enjoys building on that negotiation by asking her tenth-grade students to bring their lives, cultures, and histories to bear on larger historical and cultural events that have occurred in antiquity and on yesterday's news broadcasts. In addition to this richness of experience, Paige fills her room "with posters, student work, books, plants, and piles of things that I set down and then can't find." Arching over this assemblage of materials, ideas, and learners is Paige's belief that "all of the voices and past histories coming into play create a space that feels alive to me and changes me as much, if not more, than it changes any of my students."

As she described it, the project depicted here is part of a larger exploration in which "US history and personal history collide." Students start by examining their own culture and end by looking at that of someone else. Somewhere

a flux of cultures negotiating a common space

Dialogical Writing in Paige's Project

- Writing short reactions to text
- Charting characteristics of graphic novels
- Creating short graphic responses to prompts
- Interviewing family members about historical events
- Extending graphic novels based on interviews

in the middle, students read Art Spiegelman's *Maus* as a means of getting a sense of how historical events played on the big stage affect all of us who bear witness to them. For those who don't know the book, Spiegelman, using a comic book format and animal characters, detailed how his parents survived the Holocaust and what those experiences meant for his relationship with them. It is this insertion of the personal amid the hugely political that attracted Paige to the text. Well, that and the pictures.

As they read *Maus*, Paige had students respond to a series of generic writing prompts (e.g., What stood out for you in the text? What might be effective or limiting about telling a story this way?). In this manner, students read the text as a means for understanding the complexities of the Holocaust. At the same time, they were reading to better understand the scope and constraints of the genre. They created groups and began to unpack the conventions of graphic novels and comics by analyzing a range of examples.

With the reading and discussion of *Maus* under their belts, Paige nudged the group toward experimenting with creating graphic fiction. Using specific prompts, such as "What makes a good friend?," Paige had her students write to that topic and then enhance the initial response by fleshing it out in comic book form. The purpose, according to Paige, was to learn how to best represent "others while simultaneously representing the self." Many of these initial comic efforts were generated through electronic means and were intended to show perspectives of peers even as they illustrated the stance of the author. What had begun as short reactions to text had morphed into experiences with graphic representations and eventually, as will be described next, evolved to a more complex project.

Wanting to build on the class's experience with *Maus*, Paige told students to interview family members with the intent of connecting personal experience to some larger historical event. They, however, at first struggled to see how an uncle's exploits in the first Gulf War or a grandmother's growing up in the South prior to the passage of the Civil Rights Act carried significance similar to Spiegelman's family and the Holocaust. As she dialogued with her own practice, Paige worried that the graphic novel might have been too intimidating a mentor text.

> I have been a little disappointed by the students' lack of excitement in interviewing their family members. I tried to tell them that even though most of us are not Holocaust survivors, we are still impacted by the political, social, and economic trends that take place in this country. It has been a little difficult to convince students that their stories are valid.

However, through patient support, Paige enabled students to see how tales from being stationed in Vietnam or of a family's journey to the United States connected personal lives to the ongoing historical themes of war and immigration.

Working off the interviews, students developed a range of graphic fiction that depicted the life experiences of people they knew juxtaposed with larger historical events of the last fifty years. Using both traditional hand-drawn representation and a variety of comic software programs available online, tenth graders in Paige's class married individual and social historical events within a writing genre coming into its own. Over the course of several weeks, students went from being consumers of historical texts to assuming the stance of historians.

Working with students just entering adolescence, Emily Pendergrass approached an exploration into the qualities of leadership in a way that, similar to Paige's class, connected historical events to local understandings. As Emily described it, her project with students at West Valley Middle School grew from "an organic level of interest," bubbling up from discussions on leadership and connections to content being taught in other classes. What stands out to me about Emily's situation is that it illustrates well what Shor (1992) has identified as the three agendas that clamor for attention in all classrooms: the imposed agenda of educational expectations from policymakers and the community; the teacher's agenda of what she believes needs to be taught; and the student agenda of what they want to learn.

West Valley is a one-level, metal-roofed building that spiders out from a central core. The prime farmland around the school is being turned up and divided into home lots at an amazing pace. According to Emily,

> The scenery surrounding the school is perhaps the biggest indicator of how the neighborhood has transformed. As little as four years ago, the view was a sheep pasture and a lake. Today, the school is engulfed by million-dollar homes and an upscale golf course.

In 2000, three-quarters of the school population qualified for free or reduced lunch. However, in 2009, that percentage was barely one-third. As might be expected, such rapid change raises issues about class differences, particularly as more ability grouping in the guise of advanced and gifted classes takes place.

In this setting, Emily is the language arts teacher for students who, mainly through testing, have been deemed to be at risk of failing standardized assessments of reading. By volunteering rather than being forced into this teaching situation, Emily brings a welcoming and supportive spirit to the classroom. She creates a community in which the mutual sharing of ideas and opinions is the norm and fills the space with print and audio books, magazines, and comfy furniture to facilitate the independent reading time she offers daily. She honors the individual voices of students even as she encourages them to become a mutually supportive learning community.

Dialogical Writing in Emily's Classroom

- Individual written responses to issues raised through reading discussions

- Group charting of characteristics of leadership found in various texts

- Extended essay based on sticking points culled from earlier dialogues

This last point, honoring students and creating community, figured into an exploration based on this driving question: What are the qualities of a good leader? To broaden her students' concept of leadership, her class read pieces written by current and former gang members. In one excerpt, a gang member mentioned how much she had been affected by reading *The Diary of Anne Frank*. This admission prompted interest by Emily's students to read the classroom classic. It's at this point that the convergence of the three agendas rose before her. She was charged by the school to ready struggling readers for mandated assessments; she wanted certain objectives met and materials used during the exploration of leadership; and her students were excited about reading a book that might or might not connect to that question.

Emily decided to trust the dialogic process. Admitting that there wasn't enough time to read all of *The Diary of Anne Frank*, she brought in excerpts and a version of the play. In conjunction with this reading, Emily immersed the group in the explorations of leadership just prior to and during World War II. Students dialogued about Adolf Hitler and Franklin Roosevelt in terms of their qualities as leaders. Not wishing for her class to rely on cardboard images of these two men, Emily used questions that encouraged them to look across Hitler's and Roosevelt's accomplishments to see how complex leadership is. For example, Emily wondered aloud about Roosevelt's decision to intern Japanese Americans, a question that led to a vivid discussion among her students as, sadly, many of them had no idea that such events had occurred.

As her class read more about Anne Frank, Emily used the question of leadership as a lens for understanding the book. Rather than seeing Anne Frank's chronicle solely as a documentation of a young girl's coming of age or of the terrors of the Holocaust—both of which are of significance and value to young readers— Emily also urged her students to consider what qualities of leadership could be found in the text. In such a light, Anne's father emerged as the main leader, while other characters seemed less so. The class agreed that Anne was a leader coming into her own because she frequently spoke her mind, argued her opinions, and tried to persuade others into action.

All of the written and spoken dialogue culminated in student-written essays about some issue—a "sticking point," as Emily calls it—that stood out to them regarding leadership and their investigation of World War II. As is the case with many of the projects already described, Emily was able to have students use a range of shorter, focused writing efforts to fuel a more extended piece designed to help students bring greater shape to their thoughts. By nudging students to consider more than the obvious, she enabled them to devise a wider and many-hued palette for understanding.

Unlike West Valley, Fox River Middle School has long been centered in the congested and racially diverse eastside metro area of Atlanta, a suburban sector crisscrossed by interstates, strip malls, and chain restaurants. However, much like Emily, Lisa Hall has been involved with a population of students who are frequently shunted aside in schools. In Lisa's case, she is a language arts inclusion teacher. With the aid of a special education co-teacher, Lisa teaches classes that include many students with learning disabilities. For instance, in the class spotlighted in this segment, six of the twenty-six students required the direct support of the special education co-teacher.

Also like Emily, Lisa creates a welcoming space for students. With obvious pride, she points out that her classroom is so papered with supportive materials for students that during a state-mandated standardized test, she had to cover more of her walls with butcher paper than any other teacher in the school. In particular, student work abounds—"body biographies, heart maps, 'I'm from' narratives, and 'best part' poems"—as well as artifacts from her own life and family that she willingly shares with her students. Similar to Ian, she morphs the furniture in the room to meet the needs of her lessons, keeping the energy in the room dynamic.

> Anything that might spark a conversation about a book or a place I've visited or experience I've had, I put up in my room. I never know what my kids will be interested in, and I want to be ready for their questions and to build that relationship.

As did a number of the teachers profiled earlier, Lisa began her project by asking students to consider both their lives and the literature around them, to dialogue with themselves and with texts, the intention being to understand both better. Her specific goal was to have students develop "Where I'm From" narratives that would also be illustrated with photography. However, rather than just asking students to write a poem that connected them to their families and be done with it—yet one more hour of class time filled—Lisa used many systematic support activities to help them build richer narratives. The project became more dialogic as she layered a number of writing and reading activities in ways that had the work resonating.

Dialogical Writing in Lisa's Project

- Graphic organizer to help students brainstorm images and events from their lives

- Extended poetic narratives building from the graphic organizers and illustrated with photos

A strong believer in the use of mentor texts, Lisa got her students to page through books with "bold, beautiful pictures" like Bryan Collier's *Uptown*, Cynthia Rylant's *Something Permanent*, and Wendy Ewald's *The Best Part of Me*. Her intent was to get her students to imagine the possibilities of bringing text and image together. Having a sense of what others had done, students filled in a graphic organizer that had them brainstorming favorite places, memorable

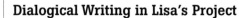

people, traditional foods, family stories and sayings, and favorite things. She was, as I've heard so many published writers advise, helping students to fill up their well of writing. But Lisa wasn't happy with just the initially brainstormed lists. Instead, she nudged and cajoled students into expanding and enriching their initial thoughts.

The exploration continued. Students wrote in extended ways about a vivid memory; using the poem "Describe Somebody" by Jacqueline Woodson, they met in pairs and word-sketched each other, and some made found poems from their memory-writes. Through all the short pieces, Lisa was getting students to make meaning of text, of themselves, and of their worlds in ways both deep and broad. With the intent of adding pictures to their narratives, students developed storyboards that helped them imagine the combination of text and image. Many were able to use disposable cameras, bought by a small classroom grant, to illustrate their writing, while others made do with photos from home or off the Web. Eventually, after many conferences and focused support, students in Lisa's class committed their narratives and accompanying photos to computer slides. The entire project culminated in a "coffeehouse" sharing, complete with hot chocolate and cookies.

Being as reflective as she is, Lisa was probably thinking about the next iteration of this project even as she was completing this one. Perhaps the hardest component was providing enough support for students over time. Despite having the special education teacher in the room, conferencing students proved challenging and taxing. When doing this project or others like it in the future, Lisa plans to "call in volunteers for conferences, so more of my students can talk about their projects more often with an adult." That concern noted, Lisa believes that the time spent developing the project was more than worth the effort expended.

> The thing that was most satisfying for me was the opportunity to give my students a place and time for individual voice. I learned things about my students I would never have learned outside of the project. For instance, I learned Joey loves to fish, and I learned about his relationship with his dad. I didn't know he was taken from his mom.

As is surely the case here, each classroom dialogue points toward the next.

To What End?

When I was coordinating a small learning community, I remember a conversation I had with a group dynamics consultant who was helping us develop better communication systems among the faculty. We teachers knew how to talk with students; we weren't as well versed in how to talk with one another, particularly in productive and supportive ways. In the course of the conversation, I mentioned the struggles students were having with one or two teachers in our program and how

I wished I could bring in other teachers more willing to dialogue. The consultant smiled. "Bob," she said, "every manager always wants to put together the best team they can, but the reality is that we usually only have the team we have. The really best managers find ways to get the most out of that team."

The seven teachers I've profiled so far and the five I'll profile in the next chapter are the best of managers. There isn't one among them who isn't hemmed in by limitations of some sort, who doesn't have a standardized test, too many students, an unforgiving schedule, or some other set of obstacles that makes teaching difficult. Each labors within the walls of ability tracking and must account with much too much regularity for standards, and lesson plans, and the like.

But rather than retreating to the faculty lounge to complain over bitter coffee, they instead accept the given circumstances and try to work within and stretch them as much as they can. I'm not arguing for the acceptance of unjust and inequitable working conditions. Those of us who are educators should always work toward the best situation for education at any given moment. However, even as we call injustice into question, we need to do our best teaching within whatever frame we currently teach. As the poet Robert Frost suggested, "You have freedom when you're easy in your harness." And so it is for the creative teacher.

By examining the standards and the tests and the other elements of their teaching contexts, the teachers in this chapter find ways to make dialogical teaching sing in their classrooms. More important, they make their teaching philosophies come alive. Soria's and Kristi's establishment of relationships, Emily's and Lisa's belief in community, Paige's willingness to take critical stances, Trevor's expectations for engagement, and Ian's insistence that learning is generative aren't just empty words on file in the recesses of some hard drive. Instead, they realize their beliefs in the classroom by designing dialogical projects that embrace and thrive on those beliefs.

The many ways these teachers used writing throughout their projects were key to keeping the work shifted to the dialogical side of the continuum. From short bursts of spontaneous reaction to extended pieces based on multiple reflections, students remained engaged with the classroom explorations because they were using writing to help make meaning. As intended, one day's writing flowed from that of an earlier day and pointed toward writing to come. Rather than seeing the literacy classroom as a hodgepodge of disconnected assignments, students began to grasp how what was written one day influenced their writing perhaps two weeks down the road. Learning became something that moved toward thoughtful wholeness rather than splintering

Questions You Might Ask Yourself

- How might I adapt the projects outlined here for my teaching context?

- How might I use more dialogical writing in my classroom?

- From my stance, what makes writing and other classroom practice dialogical?

shards of frustration. By purposefully nesting writing assignments one inside the other like Russian dolls, Kristi, Soria, Ian, Trevor, Paige, Emily, and Lisa created opportunities for resonant and rich dialogue within and across the multiple dialogical projects they and their students undertook.

I ask you to do the same. If taking a dialogical stance seems too distant from your current practice, you might try replicating one of the projects discussed herein just as it is. But don't stop there. Reflect on what occurred and spin off a variation. Or take something you've done in the past and rethink it through a dialogical lens. Better still, think about the general characteristics of all of these projects—the conversation between the personal and the academic, the opening to multiple perspectives, the reflection and engagement across time and space, the opportunities for meaning making—and develop a custom-made project tailored to the needs, frames, and possibilities of your classroom. Go ahead. Give it a shot. I've got to set up the next chapter anyway.

Chapter Five

Considering Dialogical Assessment

I f I had been a student walking into Amy Wilson's classroom at Wasatch Valley Middle School, I might have been distracted by the orange-and-green shag carpeting on some of the walls. I suspect that artifact of seventies architecture would have been hard to miss. Yet the distraction would have lasted only a few moments. Over the din of young adolescents shuffling toward desks, I would hear music playing, perhaps a movie sound track or some tune indicative of a time period or region about to be studied. Prints of art hanging in London's Tate or Philadelphia's Museum of Art might have caught my eye, if I wasn't scanning the entire back wall dedicated to work my peers and I had produced. Surely, at some point, the display linking film and print literature, with its vivid posters of movies, such as *The Fellowship of the Ring* or *Spider-man*, would have captured my attention. As my peers and I began to settle into our seats, I would have checked out today's framing questions; one focused on content (e.g., What social problems are prevalent today and how can I address them?) and a second on process (e.g., What strategies can help me understand what I read?).

With my notebook out and the music playing in the background, I'd begin to respond to what Amy calls "jump-starts," short pieces of writing that connected to concepts or themes we were currently investigating. Sometimes the jump-start would have us focus on the craft of writing (e.g., Describe your favorite dessert in mouthwatering detail), and other times we would be asked to reflect on our lives (e.g., Please describe a time that your actions had consequences, good or bad). But always, the jump-start would precipitate an extended dialogue about whatever we were currently studying, finding some way to connect our lives to the academic work.

If I finished my writing before others in class, I might go back to the book corner and browse the many graphic novels, magazines, comics, and YA fiction, or just take a moment to read through the responses that Amy had written on yesterday's jump-start. Her comments were always meant to get me thinking about what I had written and nudge me to think some more. In a reflective moment, I might have wondered how Amy had taken a room with no windows and no air conditioning and made it feel so welcoming.

Even in this brief description of the first ten minutes of a typical class, Amy's sense of purpose, of connection, and of invitation to dialogue comes through. She is aware that everything she does—from what she hangs on the walls to what she expects students to do—sends messages to learners, and she wants those messages to be coherent and valued. One clear message is that the worlds her students live in have worth in her classroom and also provide scaffolding toward understanding the academic content taught there. Yet, as much as Amy values the lives her students lead, she wants them to understand that there are lives and cultures beyond their school and community and those, too, must be valued. Another message is that in this class we write, talk, and read to make meaning both individually and collectively. Connected to that thought is the idea that we do activities in here with purpose and intent, and that all is done to further our ability to come to richer understandings. The overall tone is one that suggests both seriousness and celebration.

At least to this point, what we see in Amy's class is not substantively different from what we'd see in the classrooms of the seven teachers just profiled in Chapter 4. She, like they, advocates various ways to use literacy and the classroom context to create and extend academic dialogue. It's what comes after these first ten minutes—the degree and extent to which Amy and the four other teachers discussed in this chapter have embraced and implemented dialogical writing practice—that bears attending to. In each of the profiles to come, the focus is on seeing dialogue as core to the way learning occurs and how students and teachers can not only develop deeper understandings of content, but can also self-assess the quality and depth of their own understanding. By engaging in extended dialogues with students, Amy Wilson, as well as Angela Dean, Dawan Coombs, Sarah Skinner, and

Russ Turpin, routinely invites her students to be meaning makers and supports them in their efforts. More important, Amy and the other teachers view assessment as part of the ongoing work of dialogical classrooms.

Assessment as a Dialogical Process

In many of my teacher education classes, I ask the following question: Why do we assess? A wide range of response spills out. "Because we have to" is, sadly, a bit too prominent. "To know if students learned the material" and "to see how well we taught the material" usually follow close behind. "Reporting to parents," "covering our tails," and "diagnosing problems" figure into the mix. Although valid, all these responses tend to be either skewed toward pathology—something is wrong that must be fixed—or toward stratification—attempting to document who has demonstrated greater or lesser knowledge or ability. Furthermore, in all of these cases, assessment is an action done to students, not necessarily for or with them.

What rarely makes this brainstormed list—and if it does, it's almost an afterthought—is the belief that students can learn through assessment; that a well-planned assessment is not only cumulative but also formative, and that assessment, in the words of Grant Wiggins (1998), is educative. That's the challenge that Wiggins offers: to construct assessment from which teachers can not only gain a sense of the depth of students' "enduring understanding" of key concepts (Wiggins & McTighe, 2005), but also help learners to enhance those understandings. Equally important is that such assessment frequently involves students in the process, and that educative assessment practice engages learners, to a certain degree, in a process of self-assessment.

The idea of self-assessment is significant because it fosters self-empowerment. If assessment is always something done to us rather than with us or by us, it will rarely ever be for us. Nor will it provide us with the skills to call our own abilities into focus. We remain, for the most part, at the mercy of the judgment of others. Unless learners are engaged in the process, assessment remains largely monological.

The monological tendencies of assessment are also seen too frequently in the dynamics of classrooms. In a dialogical classroom, curriculum, instruction, and assessment need to remain in transaction; what we teach, how we teach, and how we assess what we teach should be constantly shaping and informing one another in ways that, in the end, come out more or less equally. Too frequently in too many classrooms in the United States, assessment has dominated the conversation and shifted toward monologue what should be

Qualities of Dialogical Assessment

- Educative

- Performance-based

- Includes opportunities for self-assessment

- Springs from dialogue with curriculum and instruction

- Reflects the ongoing dialogue and contexts of the classroom a dialogue. In such cases, in addition to being one-sided, pathological, and stratifying, assessment becomes primarily punitive.

It doesn't have to be this way. Assessment can be a dialogical process, one that offers supportive feedback, raises intriguing questions, and sets realistic goals while engaging teachers and learners simultaneously. As we pick up the description of Amy's dialogical classroom and follow through with descriptions of Angela's, Dawan's, Sarah's, and Russ's classrooms, first keep in mind how their work adheres to the dialogical framework previously discussed. Note how the projects in this chapter, like those in Chapter 4, are an intersection of personal and academic writing, invite many perspectives to come into play, invoke engagement, and foster meaning making. However, also pay attention to the various ways assessment is intertwined throughout the projects and how that assessment transacts with the curriculum and the instruction. Then feel free to travel back to Chapter 4 to see how assessment was also engaged in similar ways in those projects, just to a lesser extent. But do that later. Finish this chapter first.

Extended Dialogical Projects

Wasatch Valley Middle School, home to Amy Wilson's classroom, is located in the suburbs of Salt Lake City, Utah. The student population and faculty are more than 90 percent White, with a small Latino and/or Native American demographic. Having her day wedged into eight forty-seven-minute periods, Amy still managed to create dialogical engagement in her classes, which were mostly, in the language of the school, honors or average-tracked students. The single-level brick edifice of Wasatch Valley is well maintained, if a bit nondescript, and sits on a broad campus overlooking the valley. As indicated on the school's website, WVMS takes pride in the fact that it fully implements the State Core Curriculum.

Part of that core curriculum involved using the Six Traits Scoring Rubric for writing. Amy cites her desire to have students practice using the rubric as one of the reasons for embarking on the extensive autobiography project described next. By engaging her students in writing about themselves while also having them interact with a rubric, Amy created a project that fulfilled many purposes. Introducing the rubric early suggested to students that there were expectations for the writing, but clearly revealed them up front. Thus assessment was transparent and not a mystery. Using autobiography allowed her to immerse students in literature with a focus on content and also on craft. Students read mentor texts to generate working definitions of autobiographical writing. Encouraging students to tell the stories of their lives provided them with abundant sources for writing, which made it easier to extend the project. These stories also gave Amy richer insight into the lives of her students, enabling her to better support them as individuals. Knowing that the project would take time, Amy understood that it needed to pay off educationally in a variety of ways.

To pull off this project, Amy divided the autobiography into six chapters—heritage, family, elementary years, middle school years, self, and future—and provided reading and writing support for each one. For example, to get students writing about their families, Amy ran them through a series of jump-starts all focused on that topic: what is a family; please describe the pets you have or the pets you want to have; tell me about a brother, sister, or close cousin or friend; please describe a parent or other adult who has been close to you. Such writing served to fill the writing well of each student and helped him or her to see that longer writing is really just a series of shorter efforts deftly connected.

As students began to develop the jump-starts into a cohesive chapter, Amy did activities that helped students to revise as they wrote. Wanting to promote vivid description, Amy implemented a partner activity using a collection of black-and-white photos she had gathered. As she told it,

> Students each chose one picture and wrote a brief descriptive narrative about the photograph. Then, students exchanged their narratives with a partner who had not seen the photograph, and the other student tried to re-create the photograph based on the descriptive narrative that the first student had written. The students then switched the drafts of their chapters with their partners and participated in a similar activity in which the other student had to evaluate if the chapter "painted a picture in their mind" of the first student's family.

In this very subtle use of peer conferencing, Amy's students first practiced and then put to use a specific revision activity that resulted in more meaningful feedback for the young writers.

Continuing with revision work, Amy had her learners read a beautifully textured passage taken from the work of Jamaica Kincaid, one in which the author uses a rich variety of sentence length and structure to tell the story of picking bananas with her father. Rather than lecturing her students about what makes for strong sentence fluency in a piece of writing, Amy asked her students to unpack the Kincaid passage. In the ensuing discussion, they noted how by varying the sentence length, making strategic use of conjunctions, and beginning sentences with different words and phrases, Kincaid created a sense of flow in her writing. Moving from Kincaid's text to their chapter drafts, students circled all their sentence beginnings and charted sentence lengths. Armed with these graphic indicators, Amy's middle

Dialogical Writing in Amy's Project

• Engaged use of Six Traits Scoring Rubric

• Use of multiple jump-starts

• Responses to literature

• Development of multichapter autobiography

• Inventive and varied revision support activities

schoolers were better able to combine sentences and imagine alternate beginnings in a search for the flow demonstrated by Jamaica Kincaid.

And so it went for each chapter, a combination of shorter writings, dialogues with literature, and supportive revision activities evolving into another completed chapter for each student's autobiography. All along the way, students were involved in a series of peer reviews that engaged them with one another's texts through the Six Traits Writing Rubric, keeping them simultaneously in dialogue with their own writing, the writing of peers, and the expectations of the state. In completing the extensive autobiographies, students lived a writing process, watching it morph and shift as they went along. The completed work was both the assessment and the means for learning.

Of course, typical of Amy, the project was capped with a full period devoted to cookies, punch, and reading one another's autobiographies. Even here, in this culminating activity, the dialogue continued. Again, in Amy's words,

> I had stack upon stack of different colors of sticky notes piled on a table. Using these sticky notes, students commented on one another's autobiographies. They did not evaluate them, but instead just responded to them. For instance, one student had shared how his mom had died, and another student wrote a sticky note about how he was shocked when he had learned his own mother had died, too.

Surely, in Amy's classroom, these students had come to understand that writing was something each of them owned, that it had meaning for them, and it was a way to connect to others. All that, and also enough craft to meet the needs of the state assessment.

Amy's Wasatch Valley Middle School has a manageable population of around 1,000 students. Angela Dean, however, teaches in the burgeoning suburbs of Atlanta and her high school, River Park, routinely crests above 3,500 students each year. Somewhat reflecting the demographics of the county, River Park is on the verge of becoming a minority majority school, meaning that the combined minority population—African Americans, Latinos, and Asians—will soon be more than the White population. And, as noted in Chapter 3, along with this diversity of race and ethnicity, there is also diversity in socioeconomic class status.

Given this large population, the school literally overflows. Angela teaches outside the brick-and-concrete confines of the sprawling main building in what, euphemistically, has been called a mobile learning cottage. You and I would call it a trailer. Longer than wide, the narrowness of the trailer isn't conducive to desk alignments other than straight rows, although Angela admits to having pulled off a circle of sorts with smaller classes. Like Amy, Angela does what she can to make a sterile environment more inviting and conducive to dialogical learning. Wordle posters made from the works of Susan B. Anthony, Dr. Martin Luther King Jr.,

Dialogical Writing in Angela's Project

- Writing to define concepts for self and group

- Writing to spur discussion of complex issues

- Doing carousel, jigsaw, and other such literature response activities

- Completing a resource-rich in-class essay

- Developing an I-Search paper

and Elie Wiesel help, as does the lending library she maintains with her own money. Unfortunately or fortunately, not all of her books come back to her and she needs to constantly replenish the favorites. Noting how static and institutional the bare fluorescents in the ceiling make the room, Angela, similar to Kristi Amatucci, has scattered lamps about the space to soften and warm the atmosphere.

The ninth graders in her honors class represent the demographics of the school as a whole. They also tend to fill her narrow teaching space with all of their mid-adolescence energy. Capturing that energy and putting it to the task of learning is the challenge Angela faces daily. Mostly she succeeds. One of those successes involved an inquiry into social justice issues that revolved around the reading of *To Kill a Mockingbird*.

What you need to know about Harper Lee's book is that, in southern US high schools, the book has reverential status. It is mandated by many districts and, sadly, is often offered as an example of multicultural literature. What Angela does is to give the book the respect it deserves, but to make it just one piece in a larger investigation of social justice issues. Accordingly, she begins the process by asking students to each write their definition of social justice and to then suggest examples from society that might support working toward or against social justice. She then opens discussion with the intent of generating a common working definition and folds that dialogue into an examination of McClintock's (2000) Action Continuum,[1] a description of behaviors one might model in an attempt to combat oppression. Overall, her intent is to keep students connected to their perspectives, even as she nudges them to consider other perspectives.

As with any vigorous dialogical exploration, Angela leaves herself room to improvise. For example, during a recent iteration of this inquiry unit, some in the school community were trying to establish a gay/straight alliance, which caused a wave of undercurrents to surface. Rather than close her door and assume the issues didn't follow her students into her room, Angela created an opportunity for dialogue. Though she admitted this was a "scary" act, Angela understood the need to voice the dialogue:

> I knew that some of [my students] would bring up [the issues of a gay/straight alliance], along with the words "faggot" or "gay," and I also knew that some of the kids in class would take no offense to the use of such words. The conversation that resulted was really powerful. The kids who were shocked by everyone's reaction to the club, and tired of the use of such words, had the opportunity to voice their opinions. We

talked about the meaning and power of words. We discussed how some viewed the use of "that's gay" or "you're such a faggot" as being no big deal. Surprisingly, based on the mood of the school, it went over quite well and it was an effective discussion on social justice and injustice.

Life not being a sitcom, Angela's discussion wasn't intended, in the space of a single class period, to have all of her students recognize their biases and act on that recognition. Instead, it invoked a process that insisted all had to listen to one another if all were to develop understandings. It also furthered their academic inquiry into social justice concerns.

In setting up discussions of complex issues, Angela likes to work with texts familiar to the students. This choice enables learners to concentrate on analysis because they already know what happens. In this vein, Angela screened *The Color of Friendship*, a movie she admits is "cheesy," but allowed her class to bring the Action Continuum to character study. After viewing and preliminary note taking, small groups chose a character and, on butcher paper, wrote in specific terms what they knew about him or her. Then the butcher papers were passed around so each group could add responses to all of the characters. When the paper returned to the original group, they used the collected information to trace their character's journey, or lack thereof, on the Action Continuum.

In such an activity, Angela layers the dialogue, moving from their early attempts to define social justice to a discussion of the Action Continuum to character analysis using the continuum. The writings and discussions build upon, rather than are separate from, one another. This created a seamlessness that allowed her to also integrate other texts, such as the documentary *The Children's March*, Sandra Cisneros's vignette "Those Who Don't," and U2's song "Pride," into the mix. In all cases, learners wrote responses to the texts that they then shared in discussion groups. Eventually, other small groups were created that focused on some of these texts, and a jigsaw discussion was started to better acquaint students with all of the texts (for a fuller discussion of jigsaws, see Adler & Rougle, 2005).

These many layers of written and oral dialogue led to an in-class essay, which relates to that ongoing dialogue between curriculum, instruction, and assessment mentioned earlier. Angela's choice of an in-class format and four prompts for the essay has more to do with preparing students for standardized writing assessments than it does for her preference on how best to support the writing process. But having provided students with a wealth of dialogue and information, Angela knew that they entered the essay writing session deeply prepared and engaged with the subject matter. Her four prompts were all connected to the texts and issues of social justice (e.g., How is social justice more than just a race issue? In what ways does it affect gender, class, and cultural issues? Use the examples of what we have discussed in class to support your argument). Furthermore, her students had access to their prodigious supply of notes. Once again, as we indicated with Amy's work, the assessment—in this case, the in-class essay—was part of a much longer educative process.

As Angela noted, "We jump into the novel from here." All of the earlier effort went toward the framing of *To Kill a Mockingbird*. By forefronting the discussion on social justice, Angela has pulled herself out from under what I call the tyranny of text. She was no longer just, as we English teachers so often word it, "teaching *To Kill a Mockingbird*." Instead, she used that text as one among many that helped her students to unpack the complexities of social justice in the United States. In this context, knowing what happens to Scout and Atticus was less important than having their story provide insight into the lives we currently lead.

As with the other texts, Angela had students read the novel and react to a number of prompts that helped connect them to it. For example, early on in their reading, students were asked to choose between scary neighbor, first day of school, and childhood memory for a brief, descriptive journal response. After the first three chapters, Angela introduced a "chalk talk" on the subject of poverty, with students filling her white board with comments, concerns, and questions on the topic. Deeper into the novel, students wrote monologues in the voices of characters, expressing their perspectives on the trial. Near the end of the novel, students completed a four square activity that had them drawing a scene from the novel in box one, writing a descriptive paragraph and an analytical paragraph for the illustration in boxes two and three respectively, and then generating a journal entry from the perspective of a character in the last box. Whatever the activity, Angela's intent was to keep students dialoguing with the text and what they had written earlier in the unit. Writing, although in different genres, was seen as an ongoing conversation with self, text, and peers.

To pull all the work together, Angela imagined an I-Search (Macrorie, 1988) that would focus on issues of social justice as reflected in the work of the past weeks. For those unfamiliar with the genre, an I-Search has students write about a topic that they research, but also write about their research process, as well as their reflections and understandings as a result of that process. Rather than just reporting, and too frequently plagiarizing, information, an I-Search requires students to take a stance on the topic and to consider what the project meant to them. The assessment, once more, becomes part of the learning process.

For Angela, the I-Search became a way to generate new insights about the social justice issues under discussion while also getting a sense of what students had come to understand due to all the concentrated dialogue in this multistage project. She would also get another example of their ability to generate complex text as a means of response. Having identified and investigated many issues related to social justice over the weeks of the exploration, her students would now single out one issue and develop a discussion around it that relied on texts already used in class and their ability to find other source material.

For example, a student might write on the disparate ways justice is handled across socioeconomic class boundaries. In doing so, she or he could access *To Kill a Mockingbird* while also using online sources to report inequities in incarceration rates. The resulting I-Search would simultaneously present what that student had learned about the issue, what they had come to understand about the texts used in class, what they could put into action regarding research skills, and also how well that student could communicate that learning. The yield from the project would be multiple, telling, and useful to student and teacher alike.

Such educative assessment within the realm of social justice issues is what motivated a dialogical project in the high school classroom of Dawan Coombs. She asked her juniors and seniors at Rock Crest High School, located south of Salt Lake City, Utah, "What does it mean to be educated?" The intention was to develop dialogue around the purposes, possibilities, and inequities concerning education in the United States. Using the question as a lens on her curriculum throughout the year, Dawan decided to use the project described next to help her students pull their thoughts together on the subject.

Rock Crest High School is an imposing brick structure that spreads itself across its campus. Dawan's classroom was in a newer wing and was part of a small learning community (SLC) focused on supporting students in four content areas: English, social studies, science, and physical education. The SLC reflected the racial and ethnic demographics of the larger school, with one-third of the eighty-five students being Latino and the rest White. However, when looking at the students seated in the horseshoe of desks in Dawan's classroom, a visitor would notice that only one-third of them were young women.

Like most teachers, Dawan often made teaching decisions based on practicality and availability as well as educational impact, always hoping that the first two factors never outweigh the last one. Her choice of *Tuesdays with Morrie* is a good example of such a compromise. Dawan was searching for a text that would raise issues about the importance of education without preaching at her students. She also needed a text by which her students who struggled more as readers could be engaged. *Tuesdays with Morrie*, with its short chapters and conversational style depicting a relationship between a dying professor and his former student, seemed tailor-made for her needs. Perhaps best of all, a colleague had

Dialogical Writing in Dawan's Project

- Liberal use of freewrites, journals, and chalk talks

- Rationales for writing and literature choices

- Brainstorming activities

- Reflective responses

- Thematic essay that morphed into a video essay

gotten class sets of the book via a grant and was willing to share. Such is frequently the way of schools.

Dawan set out to frame that book as a means to coalesce discussions that had been in process all year. She imagined a project that would assess what her students had come to understand while helping them to focus those understandings to their needs. In a way that I hope you now recognize as a useful pattern, Dawan used freewrites, journals, chalk talks, and other such activities to have students regularly respond with their own perspectives on the issues found in *Tuesdays with Morrie*. She was particularly careful to have students collect the short writings in a folder so that later they could think back on connections and tensions between the ideas. She understood that sustaining dialogue was more than having students write frequently; they also needed to periodically and systematically reflect across those pieces.

In addition to their own words, Dawan's classes sought quotes from other texts, songs, and images that represented issues discussed in the memoir. Beyond mere collection, students needed to write about and justify these selections. As we have seen with many teachers described herein, Dawan provided the opportunity for her students to create a data-rich environment, one that was thoroughly steeped in reflection and connection.

She also helped the class see the power of collaboration. Information and thoughts were shared through informal and formal means. One example of the latter was a theme-generating exercise. Supplying each student with a pile of sticky notes, she challenged them, individually and collectively, to devise and post at least one theme for every alphabet letter. Dawan described the results:

> Some of their ideas were obvious at first (e.g., love, loss, forgiveness), but some of the more difficult letters yielded deep thinking (e.g., *z* for zombie, as in we walk through life half-asleep, not really appreciating each moment; *t* for tension, as in the tension of opposites that pull on us as we work through what we want versus what others expect of us).

Having been furnished with this bouquet of themes, students were hard put to declare that they had nothing to write about.

Using the brainstormed themes as a lens, students went back to their writing folders and thought about what theme they wanted to focus on and what in the folder might help support that dialogue. Step one in the final project was writing an essay that argued for how the theme they selected manifested in the text and why it was also important to them. From that point, Dawan had students develop a digital literacy project that used self-generated or self-selected images, quotes from their various texts, and music to further embellish the theme. Supported by peer conferencing and a group sharing of the videos, the project compelled learners to sustain dialogue in multiple ways with themselves, texts, and others.

Significantly for Dawan, she felt that this project "made the writing process real to [my students] as they tried to assemble, time, mix, and match the words and images to find the most meaningful combinations." In having to develop the project, students were invested in a learning process that helped them to deepen and enhance their understanding of themes regarding education that they had been discussing not only during this unit but also across the entire school year. And buried in all of this learning was a rigorous, useful, and comprehensive means of assessment.

The dialogical writing projects developed by Amy, Angela, and Dawan immersed their students and them in serious academic dialogue that also embraced the personal lives and perspectives of all involved. Equally significant is that these dialogues were sustained across substantial portions of the school year and culminated in projects that assessed what students had come to understand while also helping students grasp richer understandings of those themes and concepts. In the final two teacher profiles of this book, I describe how Sarah Skinner and Russ Turpin created reflective dialogical projects that, for all intents and purposes, stretched across the entire learning time spent with their respective students. For both of them, the assessment was intended as a way for students to make sense of their own learning processes and to come to some understanding of what that learning meant to them.

Long-Term, Reflective, Dialogical Assessment

When I asked Sarah Skinner to describe her teaching space at Northeastern Heights High School, she summed it up this way:

> To put it mildly, the classroom appeared colorful, junky, busy, vibrant, and a little chaotic—but definitely interesting—and the students often commented on how this room was different than other teachers' rooms. If [students] brought in something to add to the room's "collection," it just became a part of the space.

With tables set conference-style instead of individual rows of desks, announcements and student pictures sharing corkboards, and the physical space of a small workroom rather than a large classroom, Sarah sought a tone that was either comfortably academic or academically comfortable. She tried to send the message that for our community to be productive here, we need to feel welcomed into the space.

In many ways, Northeastern Heights is a newer clone of River Park High School, where Angela Dean teaches. Significantly, however, it serves about 1,000 fewer students, although the vibrant mix of White, Black, Latino, and Asian students remains in somewhat equal proportions to the older school. Also, like River Park, the socioeconomic range of the student population swings from those who require free or reduced lunch—about one-fifth of the students—to a solid 10 percent whose families occupy the upper end of that continuum. Curiously, however, to walk the halls of the school after hours is to see little evidence that such diversity exists, the ethos of a traditional American school being so pervasive. But during the day, the diverse student body wends its way through four ninety-minute blocks of ability-tracked classes that, except for Advanced Placement courses, switch with each new semester.

Into this context, no matter what supposed ability level, Sarah introduced her "memory book" project to all of her senior classes. As might be intuited from the title, the project was designed to help students assess how far they had come in their lives and how this experience positioned them for the future. Introduced at the start of the semester, it was a project that got carried through until the close. It commenced, however, with an exploration of Anne Lamott's *Bird by Bird*, a noted book on writing done in an accessible narrative style. On one hand, the book explicitly gives advice about how to position yourself as a writer, but, on the other hand, it also implicitly demonstrates the power of a witty, well-turned narrative. By unpacking Lamott's stories, Sarah was also providing her students with an example of the genre they'd be working in.

Sarah continued this blending of literature and craft study, much as Katie Wood Ray (1999) suggested. Along the way, she had students read the "My Name" chapter from Sandra Cisneros's *The House on Mango Street*, analyzing the style and voice that led to such a vivid depiction of the narrator. In a move that, at this point, shouldn't be surprising to you, Sarah had students write their own "My Name" chapter. Still later in the year, the focus became food and poetry. Inspired after reading such works as William Carlos Williams's "This Is Just to Say," Gary Soto's "Oranges," and Seamus Heaney's "Blackberry-Picking," the maturing writers in Sarah's classroom generated poems about the influence of food in their lives.

As the students dialogued with published texts in their literature study, they also dialogued with one another as writers. Time allotted for composition work was often divided into writing time and sharing time, and the latter into informal and formal sessions. During informal sessions, students would volunteer to read a work-in-progress just to, as Sarah indicated, "get it out there." Formal sessions required a student providing copies of a draft for the whole class and then having the class respond with supportive feedback. During this time, the student whose work was being discussed became a note taker, studiously getting down all the suggestions and, only later when revising the piece, deciding what advice to follow and

Dialogical Writing in Sarah's Project

- Many opportunities to respond to and imitate literature
- Informal and formal response and feedback to student writing
- Multichaptered memoir

what to ignore. As such, a kind of assessment was introduced at midpoints in the writing process. This formal feedback session enabled the young writers to take stock of a writing piece in process and revise it based on suggestions from peers as well as Sarah.

By using such a long block of time and interspersing literature study and other curriculum requirements, Sarah immersed students in an ongoing dialogue with themselves as readers and writers, one that integrated rather than atomized her instruction. With the memory book being, in Sarah's words, "an opportunity to showcase their learning about the writing process and about themselves throughout their senior year," she was able to create a project that would assess and teach simultaneously. In creating the memory book, students were engaged in an assessment that also had them generating deeper understandings about themselves, about learning, about literature, and about the writing process.

Sarah was always particularly struck by the way students took ownership of this work. As they readied their final products, she would frequently overhear students exclaiming that they had to go back and revise early pieces because they were no longer good enough to go into the submitted draft. Having been engaged in self-assessment throughout the project, the students had become arbiters of their own accomplishments. That phenomenon, and the students' insistence on having an "open read" by inviting guests, cemented for Sarah a sense that the project, although assigned by her, now belonged to the writers.

Only an hour's drive up Interstate 85 from Sarah's Northeastern Heights, Arcadia High School, where Russ Turpin teaches, seems far more distant in terms of wealth, congestion, and diversity. A rural school serving mostly working-class and working-poor families, the vast majority of which are White, Arcadia houses its nearly 800 students in a line of loosely connected wings. The main entrance is dominated by an imposing columned portico reminiscent of southern plantation architecture and Greek temples. Like many rural communities in the United States, Arcadia County has been hard hit by the recession and the upsurge of methamphetamine use. Still, the rolling hills and farmers' fields remind any visitors to the area of the need to preserve this less complex way of life before it all succumbs to urban sprawl and the ills of modern living.

Similar to Ian in the previous chapter, Russ is wont to arrange his classroom as the teaching situation dictates. Frequently students are in groups or arranged in three rows across a center aisle and facing one another. This latter arrangement seems to facilitate silent sustained reading. More often than not, groups find their way into the hall or to what they call "The Box," the foyer to Russ's wing. Regardless

Dialogical Writing in Russ's Project

- Slew of opportunities to respond to and explore various genres including essays, poetry, music, and manifestos

- Development of a multigenre project

of where they are, the students are engaged in some project that drives the learning in the classroom. All this movement is done with purpose, as Russ pointed out: "Given the variety of crazy things that we do in class, we're constantly changing our arrangement. We might stay put for a week or two, but then I like to move around. It gives students different perspectives of the classroom, and allows them to sit near students they might not ordinarily associate with."

In his Who Are You or WAY project, Russ seeks to have students make the connections between their out-of-school and in-school selves. When explaining his purpose behind WAY, Russ noted:

> The ultimate goal is to have students make multiple meanings about their entire tenth grade year, with themselves being the center. They're writing about themselves, what they've learned, and how their experiences in the tenth grade have played into all of that.

Like Sarah's memory book project, the WAY project stretches across the entire time Russ teaches his students, in this case, the school year. And, similar to Sarah, Russ finds means to integrate his varied curriculum requirements into the WAY project. But where Sarah's project is in the style of a classic memoir, Russ has his students experiment with a multigenre project.

Largely pioneered by Tom Romano (1995, 2000) and patterned after literature works (for example, see Michael Ondaatje's *The Collected Works of Billy the Kid* [1970]), a multigenre project is much like it sounds. Instead of writing in one genre—say, an editorial or a monologue—students are encouraged to blend several genres together, perhaps a short story in which some haiku, a suicide note, text messages, and radio commercials all play a part. Key to a multigenre project, and something that sets it aside from a portfolio, is that the genres need to work together to tell a complete story or develop a full argument. Leaving out one of the genres would be akin to not finishing an argument.

To facilitate writing a multigenre project, Russ has his students exploring genre across both semesters. Found poems; odes, both silly and serious; visual essays, personal essays, and editorials; a raft of short stories; longer works such as *Antigone, Schindler's List*, and Elie Wiesel's *Night*; six-word memoirs; a soundtrack-of-my-life compilation—all found their way into an ongoing discussion of genre and what characterized each genre. At one point, Russ had his students write a manifesto of sorts called "What I Want My Words to Do to You." Based on the like-titled documentary by Eve Ensler, author of *The Vagina Monologues*, and her work teaching women in a maximum security prison, this assignment is pretty much what it indicates: an honest, in-the-face assessment of the power of words and how the author hopes his or her words will affect others.

The actual Who Are You project attempts to have students make sense of what they learned both in and out of school during their tenth-grade year and how that learning has helped shape them. At the core of his intentions, Russ has invited his students into the assessment process, getting them to weigh in on the impact a year of formal and informal learning has had on them. Just by assigning the project, Russ has communicated that he isn't, and shouldn't be, the only person coming to some understanding of who they are as learners. Simultaneously, in replicating genre, the class members display their understandings of the characteristics of that genre and further immerse themselves in an ongoing and literate dialogue.

> **Questions You Might Ask Yourself**
>
> - How can I make the assessment in my classroom more educative and dialogical?
>
> - What can I do to make my practice more seamless?
>
> - What do I want my teaching to do for my students?

As suggested by Wiggins (1998), Russ—like Amy, Angela, Dawan, and Sarah—has developed an assessment that connects students to their learning processes and engages them with, rather than distances them from, their burgeoning adolescent selves. The assessments assembled in this chapter are educative in that they instruct through process. None of the culminating projects described herein suggests that the learning is finished and now let's see what you know. Instead, the assessments are all couched in contexts that emphasize that the learning process continues, that they teach even as they assess, and that they include both learner and teacher in determining what has and will continue to be learned. In short, the assessments are dialogical.

Two Vignettes

Rather than bark at you again what I've already reiterated, I instead close this chapter with two quick glimpses into the lives of teachers and students. The first inside glance takes us back to Amy and her autobiography project at Wasatch Valley Middle School. You need to imagine a living room and Amy curled up on a couch. It's two in the morning and *The Titanic* is flickering on the television screen. Piled around her are the autobiographies she has collected from her students. According to Amy,

> I was just sobbing, sobbing, sobbing. *The Titanic* didn't help the tears, but the tears were mostly caused from reading my students' autobiographies, which included stories of death, eating disorders, family suicides, family drug addictions, and other powerful narratives.

Amy, in describing this scene to me, was quick to point out that students had total control over what they would share and wouldn't share. Yet, as so often happens, most opted to share, despite the complexity of doing so.

But it wasn't only tears. The gawky silliness of early adolescence clearly erupted from the pages.

I also remember laughing. For instance, a student wrote about himself that his greatest strength was that he could eat an Arby's hamburger in one bite. Another student wrote that he would win the Nobel peace prize for turning fish droppings into a renewable energy resource.

There, long past the middle of the night, Amy was in dialogue with her students, developing understandings of them as they had developed better understandings of themselves in completing the project she had brought to them. By deeply immersing her students in a lengthy project, she had them making meaning of academic content as they made meaning of their connections to that content. In doing so, Amy was yet again reminded that she "had amazing students with rich and textured lives that extended beyond what I saw of them in school."

The second of these quick looks comes from the classroom we left only moments ago. In completing Russ's WAY project, a student I'll call Liza wrote the following paragraph:

> Mr. Turpin has had the cruelest impact on my tenth-grade career. He has put obstacles that I have never wanted to cross and never would until he put them there. He asked the questions that hurt the most, the ones that I had ignored for years because of the pain that was attached to them. He did all of this without really realizing he was doing it. He asked simple questions that to others might be meaningless. He did all of these things without even knowing the pain he made me face. It is safe to say that this man has taught me more about who I am now then he even knows.

Liza had used her WAY project to confront her many conflicting feelings about her brother's suicide. Nothing in Russ's assignment compelled her to; nothing said that she couldn't. Liza elected to have that dialogue for any number of reasons, not the least of which concerned the multiple opportunities Russ had provided her with during the year. As Liza indicated, the questions he asked were simple and straightforward. She used them to dialogue with the pain that had gripped her life for four years.

Teachers are not psychotherapists and our job is not to heal. However, our job is to, as E. M. Forster (1921) suggested, "only connect." More pointedly, as Forster continued, our job is to help our students "connect the prose and the passion" (p. 214). Liza, perhaps more than others, did just that. Importantly for her, she accepted what she characterized as Russ's "challenge of being honest in all parts of your writing." In doing so, she self-admittedly freed herself from an "entire life with all of these horrible thoughts and memories in my mind haunting me like a ghost that would never go away." A simple writing assignment, I suspect, won't be enough to keep her personal tragedy at bay forever. But it did give Liza respite for the moment and promised ways to write herself through the pain in the future. Connected to the prose and the passion, she had come to understand the power of writing.

Note

1. McClintock's Action Continuum describes ways of responding to events that are socially unjust. The first two actions—joining the unjust event or no response—are seen as countering social justice. The last four actions—interrupting the event, interrupting and educating, supporting the proactive response of others, and initiating proactive response—promote social justice. Interestingly, the third spot on the continuum is self-education and, depending on the intent, can be seen as either delaying or fostering social justice.

Chapter Six

What Do We Want?

In his book *Reading without Nonsense,* Frank Smith (2006) argued that no matter what way we teach reading, we get results. Most children learn to read. However, he asked, what kind of readers do we want those children to be? For that's where the difference lies; not all reading instruction leads to readers with the same capacities. If you focus reading instruction too narrowly on the sounding out of words or restrict understanding to plot points, you tend to create readers who see reading as an act of replication rather than one that is generative. In other words, they read for information acceptance rather than information engagement.

From a different stance, teaching reading in ways that emphasize engagement with text enables readers to develop powers of interpretation that encourage meaning making. By providing opportunities and support for doing what Lysaker (2006) has called creating relationships with text, teachers foster readers who read with purpose and focus, and who position themselves to shape and be shaped by the text. Certainly, other life events can intervene—the impact of parents, peers, or community groups, for example—but a child's developing reading experience in school contributes in powerful ways to how he or she views reading as an adult.

My sense is that writing is no different. You might, at this point, go back to Chapter 1 and re-read the introductory paragraph written by Ashley. In the excerpt, her usage, spelling, punctuation, and other conventions all adhere to the expectations of Standard Edited English. Yet Ashley herself is nowhere to be seen. She used 165 words without bringing any sense of authenticity, purpose, or direction to their employment. Rather than having language that belongs partly to others but also partly to her, as Bakhtin (1981) suggested, Ashley seems to have ceded all authority over language in this essay to some misapprehended representation of academic writing. To paraphrase an old Luther Ingram song, if writing like this is right, then I want to be wrong.

It's not that Ashley wasn't taught to write. In fact, the problem could be that she was taught, and in very specific ways regarding writing in school. For all we know, outside of a classroom setting, she might write fluid and graceful prose brimming with her many voices. However, when faced with an academic writing task, she resorts to the way that she was instructed in the classroom, a style that has handcuffed her into phrasing and word choice that feels stilted, distant, and empty. The writing that she practiced again and again in school didn't encourage her to see writing as a dialogue with herself, others, and multiple texts. Instead, it positioned her to see each writing task like a set of newly installed office cubicles: each one is the same as the others, there is little worthwhile to explore within each, and nothing is to be gained by looking in the other cubicles.

writing as dialogue with one self

You might expect me, a child of the sixties, to open the nearest window and suggest we throw this corporate metaphor through it. But let me interrupt that stereotype for a moment. For me, the entire thrust of taking a dialogical stance on writing is to acknowledge the structure and the space. What I mean is that it's not one or the other, but both; we have need for structure that imparts continuity while we have simultaneous need for openness within which to be flexible and individual.

structure and flexibility

Rather than burning the cubicles à la the open classroom movement, I have another suggestion. Instead of seeing writing through the sterility of newly installed cubicles, we should instead imagine a thriving venture space—an exciting new tech company, for instance—one populated by creative, energetic people. Within this innovative community, I implore students and teachers to stand on their chairs and look over and across all those cubicles. In doing so, they'll realize that they're all connected, that each has contributed to the structural integrity of all the others. However, by dangling over the cubicle wall, they'll see that each inhabitant, within the frame of that space, has exerted an identity of his or her own.

Through photos, knickknacks, posters, lamps, or lack thereof, the interconnected maze of cubicles exhibits both a oneness and a vibrant sense of the individual.

If we stay with this metaphor, we realize that there's room to add new cubicles, to build upon the complexity, to create larger spaces for group collaboration, and to even easily reconfigure the arrangement to meet new purposes and intentions. The physical structure is both substantial and flexible. It has a history and a present that are knowable, but leaves itself open for future iterations.

And last, in a truly innovative venture space, the people who inhabit those cubicles are valued for the knowledge and capacities they bring to their tasks. Working as individuals and in teams, their collected output constructs what the company is and will become. Concepts considered yesterday get folded into today's discussion and indicate tomorrow's dialogical directions. Nothing and no one is isolated; all contribute to an evolving sense of becoming on an individual and a group basis. Constantly in such organizations, a healthy tension exists between individual employees seeking to exert their sense of self and a corporate structure trying to present a unified concept to potential customers. It is neither one nor the other, but both engaged in sustained dialogical tension.

In a similar way, grasping the dialogical in writing is to grasp the need for individuals to remain in constant transaction with the many cultural contexts they encounter. Neither the individual nor the culture surrenders to nor compels the other. Instead, each shapes the other in a constant process of becoming. Of necessity, there is a drive toward unification; there would be no communication without it. Yet, as humans, we seek individuality. Look at schools that require student uniforms and watch how jewelry, hairstyle, and book bags call attention to the individual within the conformity. As Bakhtin (1981) has argued about language, it's neither the unification nor the individualization that matters as much as the tension between the two. It's the latter—the pull and tug between the individual and the larger culture—that encourages, indeed ferments, dialogue.

You and I have been dialoguing through slightly more than five chapters. It's my sincere hope that you haven't been either accepting or rejecting my ideas at face value, but, instead, have been raising tough questions throughout. So where do you go from here? Up to this point, I have offered definitions of dialogical writing projects, suggested qualities that facilitate such work, and provided a range of vivid examples culled from the practices of teachers who are walking the walk. To what purpose, you might ask? Two, would be my answer.

The first purpose is to discuss the implications of this work: what it might mean for teachers, teacher educators, students, parents, administrators, and policymakers to support dialogical writing in schools. You could call this a discussion of the "so what" of taking a dialogical stance. How can educational stakeholders shoulder the responsibility, and what are the possible tools for engaging dialogue on the issues?

The second purpose of this chapter—what I call the "so why"—is to remind readers of the existential and immediate need for this work and to argue that teaching writing in formulized ways for out-of-context standardized writing tests hurts students, the teaching process, and, ultimately, our society. In particular, such narrow approaches to writing demean and oppress students who through gender, race, ethnicity, sexual identity, and other sociocultural factors find themselves marginalized within the systems of public and private education at work in the United States. What I argue is, if there must be cubicles, let's provide enough for all of us and make them plenty roomy and versatile for our under-construction selves to be evident and influential on the emerging structure.

So What

Creating dialogical writing projects based on the framework projected in this book is less a *building new* and more a *returning to*. There exists in this country a rich, if sporadic, history of education that, through intent and execution, valued dialogue with text, with self, and with others. You can locate many of the ideas discussed here in the works of educators such as Paulo Freire, Ira Shor, Patricia Stock, and Martin Nystrand. And before them, John Dewey and Louise Rosenblatt argued for various forms of dialogical classroom practices. We stakeholders in education— that is to say, all of us—need to dialogue with that legacy to better conceive what current and future dialogical writing classrooms look like. So when I suggest we return to certain ideas, the intent is not to replicate whole what was done before, but instead to dialogue with those ideas in ways that bring us fresh stances on current educational classrooms and the issues that complicate them.

What is new or more immediate, I would argue, is the imperative for implementing dialogical writing projects in secondary language arts classrooms. With the flush of new media and the accessibility of wide and divergent sources of information 24/7, perhaps never has it been more necessary to develop readers and writers who dialogue with, rather than merely consume or haphazardly produce, text. Because learners have wider and more prevalent opportunities to encounter and create divergent information sources, they need to be independent dialoguers with a range of media, ones who call the texts they read and generate into question.

Crucial, too, is the understanding that the first decade of the current century was witness to a severe and, from my stance, debilitating compression of what constitutes reading and writing in schools. By teaching students to read and write in ways that keep them from engaging text in any substantive fashion is to severely handicap them and the future society they will be charged with creating. We can and must do better.

But just what am I asking educators and their attendant stakeholders to return to? **First off, we who educate must return to envisioning our classrooms through what Peter Smagorinsky (2002) has called principled practice.** We need rationales for teaching that resonate with the voices of many classrooms. *NCTE Beliefs about the Teaching of Writing* is an excellent place to start. Certainly Russ and Sarah would agree. When you visited their classrooms in Chapter 5, you saw instructional practices that were grounded either knowingly or intuitively in these belief statements. In the semester-long projects that shaped both of their dialogical projects, you witnessed how writing, when seen as a process, becomes a tool for thinking, engages complicated social relationships, connects in varied and intimate ways to reading, and is learned through doing. Choices in both classrooms were not made by whim or on the winds of some slick, expensive, and inflexible program. Instead, the practices of Russ and Sarah were steeped in the experiences of successful teachers of writing from across the country.

I urge teachers to access the *NCTE Beliefs about the Teaching of Writing* and, at the very least, imagine their classrooms through those lenses. Better still, English teachers should take these beliefs to their department meetings and suggest that, along with all the talk about book ordering and hat policies, some dialogue around professional matters might invigorate everyone. Borrowing a protocol from the Coalition of Essential Schools, teachers could discuss how much or how little they see each belief statement in practice at their school. For those principles only rarely or sometimes seen at their school, the department could collaborate on dialogical writing projects that would bring those practices closer to the forefront. Teachers having greater success in certain areas could act as mentors for those less experienced, and all could contribute ideas that have worked for them. Whatever the approach, immersion in a dialogue around these belief statements will nudge everyone's practice into more effective engagement.

Given this foundation of resonant practice, **English teachers need to return to seeing classrooms as small learning communities rather than test preparation centers.** By enacting dialogical writing projects, you can engage students in learning that draws upon all in the room to bring all of themselves to the work. Like Ian who set his students to grappling with philosophic issues related to art, poetry, and music, you can construct opportunities for learners to experience the amazing satisfaction that comes from common intellectual struggle that yields insightful results. In a similar vein, you can bring the flexibility to unit planning that Emily demonstrated, in which she found ways to incorporate student questions and interests into her class' ongoing exploration of leadership. In both cases, Ian and Emily valued their students' capacities and willingness to delve into complex issues when provided many opportunities to dialogue through connected reading and writing.

I think the best way to establish the concept of small learning communities in your school is to start with your own classroom. Communicate through word and deed to your students that you respect their ideas and value their informed opinions. The latter point is crucial; students need to take responsibility for their assertions and must be able to provide evidence from text and from experience. Without doing so, relativism rages and, Cole Porter to the contrary, anything does not go. But providing students with regular opportunities to dialogue with themselves, with text, and with others establishes ways of working in which understandings are mutually constructed. Once students grasp the power and possibilities of dialogue in your classroom, they will coalesce into a community of learners.

At that point, you can begin to invite colleagues from within and across departments to witness how using dialogical writing projects has shifted the ways in which your students and you view learning. Colleagues will be able to witness how seamless and integrated your writing and reading work has become. They'll see students writing more for the understanding writing enables and less because it's what you assigned. By connecting with your students, colleagues won't have to take your word for it; they'll be able to watch the changes occurring.

To support these colleagues in their fledgling efforts at dialogical practice, you might establish lunches away from the faculty room. In these brown bag sessions, you can co-plan and act as mutual brainstormers, devil's advocates, shoulders for commiseration, or cheerleaders for overcoming flagging energy. Having established a critical mass of teachers successfully working from a dialogical stance, you could open discussions in your school with the intention of realigning into smaller units that enable stronger classroom relationships. None of this can take place overnight, but it can and does happen when faculty members start small but dream large.

Key to creating small learning communities is to return to the idea that we should put students and meaning making at the center of our classroom activities. Think about how Amy and Dawan, through extended writing activities, asked students to connect their lives to the experiences they encountered in literature. In the autobiographies that were produced in Amy's class and the videos that discussed issues related to education generated with Dawan's facilitation, students were positioned as meaning makers, as learners capable of bringing insight into their experiences and

Practice to Return To

- Teaching from belief statements based in the work of classrooms

- Seeing classrooms as small learning communities

- Putting students and meaning making at the center

- Streamlining curriculum

- Acknowledging classroom tensions

- Taking a reflective stance on teaching

that of others. In both cases, a wide scope of support activities was provided, but ultimately each student had to use those activities to generate his or her understandings.

When I plan lessons, I generally ask myself three things as I structure the learning activities: Is this a concept that needs enduring understanding? If supported, can learners figure this out for themselves? Do I have the time to let them work through the meaning making? If I can answer yes to all three questions—and this happens most frequently—then I create or borrow a protocol that enables students to take responsibility for their own learning. A quick example is that I rarely lecture on genre. If I want students to learn about haiku, for instance, I give them access to a range of these poems. Sure enough, any group I've ever taught this way begins to brainstorm characteristics: three lines, seventeen syllables, references to nature, focus on detail, show don't tell, and the like. Oftentimes students even pick up on the nuances of haiku: brief and telling might be more important than keeping the seventeen-syllable structure, as a case in point. Having them work for their own understandings might take longer than a lecture on the structure of haiku, but they come away so much more capable of working in the genre through a close dialogue with the form.

If the lives of students and meaning making are to be centered in classrooms, then schools need to return to curricula that are streamlined and flexible. We need to avoid, as Wiggins (1989) has suggested, the futility of attempting to teach all content deemed important. It is an impossible task. Looking from a Coalition of Essential Schools (2010) stance, faculties must see the wisdom of less is more. When school district personnel overcrowd curriculum, learning gets reduced to superficial encounters. Content may get covered—taught in only the most shallow definition of that word—but it most likely won't be learned to any great depth or engagement. However, when Trevor took time to involve students in making sense of Shakespearean tragedies and Kristi immersed her classes in reading and writing narratives, all in class came away with learning experiences of depth and sustenance. To do so, both made choices. Some lesser aspect of the curriculum was jettisoned so greater focus could be placed on literature and concepts more fundamental to negotiating the field.

Although teachers can make such choices in their classrooms, they frequently do so under threat of being sanctioned by the district or even state administration. As such, individual teachers should make curricular choices with caution and transparency. Still, the streamlining of curriculum needs to occur. This is the kind of discussion that can begin in English department meetings. If most or all of the English teachers of a school agree that the body of material being taught to tenth-grade students, for example, is excessive, they might carry enough influence to get the district to reconsider. Changes such as this rarely happen quickly, but they can happen when teachers collectively enter into dialogue with a willing administration. Very often principals and language arts coordinators who are a year or two into the position—not new enough to be overwhelmed by the job, but not veteran enough to be co-opted by the system—are very approachable as they look for ways to have positive impact on classrooms.

As curriculum negotiations might imply, teaching is not without tensions. Educational stakeholders need to return to perspectives that acknowledge those tensions and seek to understand how vibrant learning can emanate from them. In confronting language stereotypes through her study of Spanglish, Soria didn't shrink from the issues, but instead deliberately explored the ways we construct identity for ourselves and others through language. When Angela investigated social justice issues with her classes, she knew that dialogues around race, class, and sexual identity might make some in her classroom uncomfortable, particularly those students whose sociocultural background tended to place them in majority status in the school. But she realized that not to have those dialogues would leave her more marginalized students in an extended limbo of discomfort, to say the least. Both Soria and Angela recognized the need to acknowledge and then unpack those tensions to better enable their students to cross cultural borders.

Acknowledging the tensions in a classroom can feel frightening, but experience has helped me frame such discussions in ways that move us all toward mutual shaping of perspectives. For me, any acknowledgment of tension falls on its face when I push for a quick solution that, in truth, replicates my take on the issue. You can see how what I've described is not dialogue. I'm assuming a side; I'm assuming a correct stance. Although it can often be difficult to do when I hear statements that I consider to be offensive, I've learned to ask questions: Why do you feel that way? What has been the extent of your experience? Do you think that response always happens? Does anyone else know of another explanation? I also offer a range of examples that illustrate the many layers of a concern. My intention has shifted from trying to have students think as I think on a particular issue; I, instead, create opportunities for all of us to think about the issue in more complex ways. I enter into dialogue to better move beneath the facile and unexamined. Rather than seeking a pat and false resolution, I seek to start a process of dialogue with complex issues that might continue past the final day of the semester.

All of these instructional shifts would be greatly facilitated if individual teachers and, more significantly, school districts returned to recognizing the importance of educators taking reflective stances on their practices. Certainly teachers, but content area coaches, principals, and central office personnel as well, would benefit from what Cochran-Smith and Lytle (1993) have called systematic and intentional inquiry into practice. Paige is an excellent example of this. Although her project using graphic novels provoked energetic involvement and vivid writing, she called that work into question, even as it was under way. Clearly, Paige believes that all instructional practice can be made better, or at least rethought in terms of changing contexts. Lisa, as a teacher coming into her own, routinely sits down with her completed projects and asks, if I were to do this again, what would I do differently? For example, her postassessment of the "Where I'm From" project indicated that having more adults handy during the conferencing and video stages of the process would provide more one-on-one support for students new to digital composing. For Paige and Lisa, taking a dialogical stance on a classroom means more than teaching students in dialogical ways. Such a stance also includes dialoguing with instructional practice.

I always recommend that teachers reflect on their practices with other teachers. Doing so brings other perspectives into the conversation and helps to break down the isolation of teachers. Certainly, any group of teachers can agree to collaborate reflectively with one another, but joining an established group can be easier in that they have a history of practice and a collection of protocols to call on. Most, if not all, of the nearly 200 sites of the National Writing Project devote some aspect of their professional development work to teacher inquiry communities. I first connected to such reflective practice through the Philadelphia Writing Project, and many of the teachers profiled within have taken part in our Red Clay Writing Project summer institutes. If schools can recognize the power of such professional learning, then grade group, departmental, and cross-departmental initiatives devoted to reflective practice can flourish, especially if schools redirect funds away from expensive consultants and one-size-fits-all programs. And, in the age of digital learning, not all reflective practice networks need be face-to-face. Through listservs, wikis, Nings, online conferencing, and who-knows-what-next technology, teachers in Soldotna, Alaska, can network with colleagues in Beaufort, South Carolina. All it takes is the will and a reliable Internet provider.

Before sliding into the "So Why" section of this chapter, I need to address one lingering issue. In working with teachers and teacher educators, I frequently notice a tendency to dichotomize, to take positions on teaching that are this or that, but never some combination of the two. Drawing on the discussion of Bakhtin (1981) earlier in the chapter, I want to argue that classrooms are healthy places when teachers recognize the tensions at play there and position themselves flexibly between the poles. So it's not teacher-centered or student-centered—one or the other forever and ever—but *more* teacher-centered or *more* student-centered depending on the classroom context at any given moment. I don't have to be dialogical at the complete expense of lecture mode, but I can decide what degree of each stance will better fit the current teaching situation this week, this day, this minute.

What comes to mind for me is a soundboard in a recording studio, that wedge-shaped console full of dials and meters where the engineer regulates the reproduction of the performance. Generally, the broad center of the soundboard is taken up by a series of sliding switches set in vertical grooves. These switches represent different points on the sound spectrum and can be set for more bass or treble depending on the recording situation. If there were eight such sliding switches on the board, each would be positioned differently relative to one another. Rarely would you see all the sliding switches set evenly in a row across the board.

I think of a classroom that way, as having sliding switches that I can manipulate to produce the best teacher performance for any given lesson. I might start the class with a journal that focuses on a more personal response from students, but could shift the switch and end the class with an activity that drew on a more academic stance, knowing that in either case some of each—personal and academic—was always present. Likewise, an initial setting might be more dialogical, but, based on time restraints, I would move part of the session into a more monological lecture and then tamp the switch back to a stronger dialogical setting to close out. Wanting individual responses to a poem, my classroom seating structure might be originally set as straight rows, but later the setting would slide more toward pairs and eventually small groups as we shared those individual responses. Thinking of classroom stances as choices and seeing them as eminently movable presents me with so many more options for classroom success. As much as I advocate dialogical approaches—I did write a book on it—sometimes both my students and I appreciate when I say, "Here's what seems to work best."

So Why

When the military forces of a country take over a government, one of their first acts is to close the universities. There is a reason for that. The military leaders want to cut off dialogue, the free and vibrant exchange of ideas. In tandem, they will also take control of newspapers, radio, and television, either shutting them down completely or severely limiting what stories can and can't be told. More recently, in places such as Myanmar and Iran, government control of cell phones, texting, and the Web have tried to prevent citizens from dialoguing via these new electronic forms of media. In all of these cases, the government seizes ownership of education and mass communication to isolate, restrict, and monitor meaning.

In the United States there has not been a military coup, but there has been a systematic attempt over the first decade of the twenty-first century to limit the ways we dialogue in schools. Through the increasing use of inflexible accountability measures, pacing schedules that deny an individual's own learning arc, decontextualized and punitive standardized testing, and incessant layering of benchmark and end-of-course tests, federal, state, and local education officials have created an atmosphere in schools that is skewed way toward the monological end of the spectrum. This is the end where meaning and understanding are controlled. As such, classrooms are seen as places where the only goals are to have students score better on the tests and to do so by any means necessary. Writing, if it is practiced at all in such classrooms, is primarily restricted to that writing which will be tested by the state. Students don't write to construct meaning; they write to achieve statistical means.

Aside from scaring the most innovative and thoughtful teachers and teacher candidates away from the classroom, such a pervasive atmosphere of control diminishes the quality of education that can occur there. When we remove the capacity for dialogue, when we speak only in an authoritative voice, Bakhtin (1981) suggests that we leave our audience only one of two options: acceptance or rejection. My fear is that too many students are opting for the latter. Those whose culture most closely resembles the dominant culture of the school might stay physically present, but, in the absence of any sincere dialogue that respects the insights and concerns they carry, they too frequently view high school as a credentialing hoop merely to be tolerated. Long past hope of engagement, these students persevere because cultural evidence suggests that, like it or not, the system works in their favor.

Worse, however, is what students from cultures more marginalized from the mainstream of school too often tend to do. Stripped of the opportunity to dialogue—to bring their voices, issues, and identities to the table—they remove themselves altogether from classrooms. In the United States, high dropout rates and financial impoverishment go hand-in-hand. With national graduation rates hovering between 65 percent and 71 percent for the years 1972–2004 (Greene, 2002; Swanson, 2004), the United States saw at least twice the number of students from low-income families dropping out of high school than those from middle- and high-income families combined. According to one source, "In 2004, the [dropout] event rate for students living in low-income families was approximately four times greater than the rate of their peers from high-income families" (Laird, DeBell, & Chapman, 2006, p. 4).

The numbers are, at best, worrisome, but at their direst they predict a continued erosion of minority participation in public education. For too many Latino, Black, and Native American students, especially if their families are working class or working poor, school is like a foreign land, one that diminishes their culture, denies their perspectives, and wishes they weren't there. Given that level of dis-invitation, they too often comply with that wish.

Questions You Might Ask Yourself

- What do I do every day to invite all students to be part of my classroom?

- What do I do every day not to replicate the ways schools have been used to oppress marginalized student populations?

- What do I do every day to make my classroom a place where it is safe to express worries, concerns, and dreams?

- What do I do every day to develop writing opportunities that, rather than being stand-alone and lifeless, create ongoing opportunities for dialogue?

However, as indicated earlier, when dialogue leaves the school, students aren't the only ones who go with it. As national control of local education initiatives increases, teacher voice in terms of curricular, instructional, and assessment decisions dramatically decreases. Compared to the final twenty years of the twentieth century in which the educational literature expected teachers to be intellectuals (Giroux, 1988), inquirers (Cochran-Smith & Lytle, 1993; Goswami & Stillman, 1987), reflective practitioners (Schön, 1983), and change agents (Fullan, 1993), the start of the twenty-first century has seen the rise of scripted reading programs, standardized curricula, and high-stakes testing (Gutierrez, Asato, Pacheco, Moll, Olson, Horng, Ruiz, Garcia, & McCarty, 2002; Kohn, 2000; MacGillivray, Ardell, Curwen, & Palma, 2004; Meier & Wood, 2004). Rather than respecting the experiences and knowledge base of teachers, these initiatives remove decision-making control from the classroom and place it into the hands of distant others.

This loss of autonomy is telling. Of teachers in the United States who leave K–12 teaching for other jobs inside or outside education, 54.8 percent and 63.5 percent respectively report that they have more autonomy on their current jobs than they did when employed as teachers (Marvel, Lyter, Peltrola, Strizek, & Morton, 2007). The same study indicated that fewer than one in five teachers who leave teaching for other jobs in and out of education felt they had more autonomy as teachers. Such numbers imply a growing sense of powerlessness among the teaching population. The voices of teachers in terms of educational decision making seem like an echo down an empty corridor.

It is difficult to ask teachers who have lost dialogue with administrators and policymakers to resurrect that dialogue in their own classrooms. Difficult, but not impossible, because that's what I'm asking in this book. What I've provided in these pages is an exploration of perspectives on teaching that can be assets in terms of implementing a dialogical classroom. By seeing learning as generative, valuing relationships among teachers and students, evolving learning communities, seeking to combine engagement and rigor, and taking a critical stance on learning, you can lay the groundwork for and sustain powerful instruction. Such teaching is rich in dialogue; it vibrates with the pulses of engaged learners and flows outward with their words. You have seen this resonance in the examples provided by Amy, Angela, Dawan, Emily, Ian, Kristi, Lisa, Paige, Russ, Sarah, Soria, and Trevor. You have sat in their classrooms; you have watched them teach.

In doing so, you have seen one quality of dialogical teaching that has gone largely unexpressed to this point. Each of the twelve has shown courage. They have weighed the complexities of creating dialogical writing projects, deemed them worthwhile, and have summoned the courage needed to implement such instruction. Each has had the bravery—the chutzpah, if you will—to slow down the curriculum, to engage students in discussions of sensitive issues, to leave these discussions open to multiple interpretations, and to encourage young writers to bring themselves to the writing in an attempt to make meaning rather than merely making do. I'm not sure any of the teachers profiled here would characterize themselves as being courageous, but, nonetheless, they are.

As Oz said to the Cowardly Lion, "I can't give you courage." I wish I could. But that's something you'll need to muster on your own. What I can and have given you is this book with its framework and examples for developing a dialogical writing community in your classroom. That classroom is one in which literacy is used to immerse teacher and students in an ongoing reflective conversation with the texts of their lives. In that classroom, you will strive to develop writing projects that (1) represent an intersection of academic and personal writing, (2) allow writers to bring multiple voices to the work, (3) involve thought, reflection, and engagement across time and located in space, and (4) create opportunities for substantive and ongoing meaning making. It is in such a classroom—your classroom—that dialogical writing flourishes.

In lieu of courage and in addition to this book, I'll leave you with this thought precipitated by the writer Flannery O'Connor (1979). In an essay on writing short stories, she ended with these lines: "You ought to be able to discover something from your stories. If you don't, probably no one else will" (p. 106). I think that quote will do well as pretty good advice to pass on to your students. Certainly, opportunities to write in dialogical ways will lend themselves to such discovery.

But I think a paraphrase is in order. I suggest that if you can't discover something in your own teaching, probably no one else will either, least of all your students. Take the time and opportunity to dialogue with your own practice. Seek the courage to dialogue in substantive ways with your students. Give them and you the infinite possibilities of ongoing, connected, and generative dialogue. Who knows what wonders may be wrought?

Writers on Writing: The Spiritual, the Profane, and the Authority to Write

I t's my belief that some of the most interesting and contradictory advice about writing and teaching writing comes from writers themselves. They can be all over the map, which is why I love to read their views. It's a dialogue stretching across the years, one that keeps forcing you to rethink your stance on what it means to write and teach writing. It is through the practitioners of the art, craft, or science of writing—take your pick, or perhaps all three—that we develop an insider's view of the complexities, possibilities, and frustrations of bringing out thoughts to the page or monitor. And in the dialogue of authors, we are again reminded that there are many ways to write and many ways to consider how we approach the teaching of writing.

For instance, **Flannery O'Connor**, writing in ***Mysteries and Manners*** (1979), didn't have much use for us teachers, or rather saw us as only useful in certain ways:

> I don't know which is worse—to have a bad teacher or no teacher at all. In any case,
> I believe the teacher's work should be largely negative. He can't put the gift into you,
> but if he finds it there, he can try to keep it from going in an obviously wrong direc-
> tion. We can learn how not to write. . . . (p. 83).

Ms. O'Connor was nothing short of opinionated, probably as vocal as the peacocks she kept on her Milledgeville, Georgia, farm. Her advice will slap you on the head and make you see stars. Complacency will shatter and be swept off the porch of your practice.

No less opinionated, but far more sensitive to the fragile needs of aspiring writers, **Brenda Ueland** was a consummate teacher of those who would put, prob-ably more figuratively these days, pen to paper. As the title to the first chapter of *If You Want to Write* (2007) indicates, "Everybody is talented, original, and has something to say" (p. 3). She also shares with O'Connor a connection to writing that is spiritual, but less Catholic and more William Blake. She argues that Blake wanted the creative spirit kept alive in all people. Because, as she answered her own question, "it is life itself" (p. 9). According to Ueland, nothing is more important; without the creative spirit, we are merely "legs and stomach, materialistic cravings and fears" (p. 9). In reading her book, you'll come to understand why the NPR commentator Andrei Condrescu in his foreword exclaimed that "Brenda Ueland is a believer and her faith is contagious" (p. xi).

If there is a theme being generated here, it's that writers make their mean-ing known. **Derrick Jensen** is no different. I use his book *Walking on Water: Reading, Writing, and Revolution* (2004) as the first text in my courses on how to teach writing. My students either love him or hate him, which is exactly what I want as we begin to dialogue about what makes for a strong and effective writing classroom. Jensen believes in the power of emotion. He teaches that way; he writes that way. You'll find yourself arguing with him, but you won't put him down.

If there's a spiritual side to Jensen's text, it comes through in his love and defense of nature. His faith, however, is in his students. He closes the book with an anecdote about a writing conference with a woman who was writing a farewell letter to her best friend moving a great distance away. After she reads the solid, but emotionally distant, letter, Jensen asks her how she feels about her friend leaving. The woman breaks down and sobs. "Put that on paper," he says (p. 213). She does, and in the conference the next day, both are so swept up by her words that neither can finish reading the letter out loud. When she can finally bring herself to talk, the student sighs, "I get it" (2004, p. 213).

As does **Anne Lamott,** who isn't one to hold back on emotion or opinion either. Invariably, one of the teachers in our annual Red Clay Writing Project summer institutes will invoke her book *Bird by Bird: Some Instructions on Writ-ing and Life* (1995). With some embarrassment, I need to admit that I haven't read all of this book. I have no need. So many sections of it have been read aloud across eight summer institutes that the book is now part of my writing spirit. It goes where I go. More portable than a paperback.

However, of the many cited sections of Lamott's book, one seems to get referenced more than the others. It strikes me as amusing that often a heretofore soft-spoken epitome of Southern politeness will rise to the full extent of her five-foot-two-and-a-half-inch frame and read with gusto selections from the chapter titled "Shitty First Drafts" (p. 22). For Lamott tells it as it is, that we need to shut off that infernal and internal, but hopefully not eternal editor as we try to get a composition rolling. We have to allow ourselves to get something on the paper or the screen in all its imperfect messiness. Although perhaps not as graphic, the rest of the book reads with that same sense of your best writing friend sitting across from you at a coffee shop alternately cheering and cajoling you toward that more perfect text.

Best known for writing and performing *The Vagina Monologues*, **Eve Ensler** is yet another writer unafraid of emotion and strong opinion. In her documentary shown on PBS and available on DVD, ***What I Want My Words to Do to You,*** Ensler gives you a seat in her writing class within a women's maximum security prison. Using a series of writing exercises as an organizing device, the video captures the way this sensitive teacher encourages the women in her class to make meaning of their lives through writing. Each of these vivid and wrenching work sessions is punctuated by one of the women reading her response to an assignment suggested by the video's title. The result is moving, soul-searching, and uplifting.

With perhaps the same intent as Ensler and certainly a nod to the spiritual connections of writing, **Natalie Goldberg** crafted an enduring handbook that writers and teachers of writing should keep near them at all times. In ***Writing Down the Bones: Freeing the Writer Within*** (1986), Goldberg uses Zen as a basis for helping writers develop the mind-set to write, for seeing the words that are inside and tugging them to the surface. Written in short chapters that can be read quickly and out of order, this book gracefully, and at the reader's pace, layers on beliefs about writing and ways of understanding the world.

Two juxtaposed chapters particularly offer a sense of the spirit and focus of Goldberg's stance. The first of the two is called "Doubt Is Torture" and tells of advice given to an aspiring songwriter from a Buddhist teacher. When the songwriter suggests that his aspirations might not work out, the teacher urges him to get up "no matter how many times they knock you down" (p. 117). As if in response to the grit of that chapter, the next one, "A Little Sweet," suggests that, like students of the Torah who are given a candy after their first lesson, writers need to associate writing with experiences in their lives that are lush and sweet and pleasant. Like Ensler and Lamott, Goldberg acknowledges the struggle that is writing and, again like those two writers, understands the richness that can be found in our efforts to put thoughts to page.

I think these writers—but really any writers who reflect on their craft vividly—demonstrate that the actual work of writing is far removed from the clinical and soul-deadening exercises that pass for writing in far too many mandate-burdened classrooms. For O'Connor, Ueland, Jensen, Lamott, Ensler, and Goldberg, writing is about finding what is unsettling us inside and getting it out there to unsettle others. It's about connecting thought and emotion to words. It's about seeing the physical and the metaphysical in dialogue. It's about bringing our past and present selves into dialogue with the people and writers we are becoming. It is, as the title of O'Connor's book intimates, about mysteries and manners.

Books Worth Returning To

I have a well-thumbed copy of Paulo Freire's *Pedagogy of the Oppressed* (1970). Sticky notes sprout from it like dry reeds in an autumn marsh. Pages lie stuffed between the battered covers with only their numbers to keep them in order. Large portions of the text are underlined or highlighted in whatever color and by whatever type of writing implement was handy at the moment. Then there are those other smudges and stains that hopefully are only the pale reminders of some long forgotten meal or snack. I have the newer edition of the book, the one with the red cover and the language degendered, but when I need to think in deep ways about teaching and social issues, this old one fills my hand and comes off the shelf.

For me, some texts are deep wells that, no matter how often you drop your bucket into their depths, it comes up full of that which is fresh and sweet and filling. *Experience and Education* (1938) by John Dewey, *Literature and Exploration* (1938) by Louise Rosenblatt, and *Discourse in the Novel* (1981) by Mikhail Bakhtin all share that exalted status. So, too, can I reread Camus, Forster, and Salinger with a renewed sense of expectation. When I watch, yet again,

Ingmar Bergman's *Fanny and Alexander*, Akira Kurasawa's *Ran*, or Francis Ford Coppola's *The Godfather, Part Two*, I find myself holding thoughts that hadn't occurred to me on previous viewings. No matter what their length, these works sit thick amid the rest of my collection.

Although not carrying quite the same weight as the works I've just mentioned, there are a number of books that I find myself increasingly turning to when I start thinking about the courses I teach or when a Red Clay teacher asks for a recommendation to inspire her practice. What I like about these texts is that they make theory come alive in classrooms by vividly showing how our beliefs about teaching writing and our teaching decisions are in constant and evolving dialogue. Each is neither a grab bag of teaching tricks nor a snooze of theory. Instead they resonate with the way theory and practice talk to one another in effective classrooms.

Narrative Writing: Learning a New Model for Teaching (2007) by **George Hillocks Jr.** is an excellent example of this conception. As he and his University of Chicago MAT students worked in urban schools, they brought narrative writing to the forefront because "it serves both as a basis for later writing in other genres and as a foundation for the study of literature" (p. 30). What I particularly like about this book is that it chronicles how he and his students troubleshoot their teaching, so they not only model writing activities, but also illustrate how teachers can call their practice into question in ways that refine and evolve it. And I continue to use this book with preservice teachers because it champions the way narrative plays out in all genres, useful knowledge to retain in expository heavy high schools.

Perhaps something all these books have in common is the concept of modeling theory-based practice. Such is certainly the case with **Katie Wood Ray's** *Wondrous Words: Writers and Writing in the Elementary Classroom* (1999). The reason I can recommend this book geared for teachers of young children to middle and high school educators is precisely because the theory that drives her practice is so sound and flexible. Her idea is simple enough: What does it mean to read like a writer? By looking at the craft of experienced authors, those who are less experienced can learn much about how it's done. Ray likens it to a friend who, as a seamstress, doesn't go to stores to shop for clothes, but trawls the aisles turning skirts and dresses inside out looking for "*idea*s for clothes" (p. 13, italics in original). As a teacher of current and future secondary English teachers, I like using Ray's book because if third graders can read with an eye for craft, we should certainly expect seniors to be able to do the same.

That immersion in text carries through *Writing in Rhythm: Spoken Word Poetry in Urban Classrooms* (2007). In this book, **Maisha Fisher** documents how Joe Ubiles and his Bronx high school students dubbed Power Writers resonated with the words and tempos of popular culture as they sought to create visions of urban life. At the center of this work is a multicultural classroom where all who entered that zone of language exploration "cocreated traditions around words, sounds, and power through their poetry" (p. 4). What stands out to me in this text is how well Fisher brings not only the classroom to life on these pages, but the theory that supports the practice as well. And, if it does nothing else, her text reminds us how powerfully words and ideas flow through the pens of young, engaged minds under the facilitation of a caring, sensitive adult.

Those engaged minds are certainly in evidence in the classroom of **Jeff House**, although lodged in California, a continent away from the Bronx. In ***Writing Is Dialogue: Teaching Students to Think and Write Like Writers*** (2006), House argues for taking an inductive stance on the teaching of writing to commence, as he notes, "a rummaging of the cabinet in search of something to cure what ails us" (p. 4). To write inductively is to gather particulars with the intent of identifying patterns and eventually creating a cohesive work. Aspiring and veteran teachers in my classes enjoy this book because the theory and practice talk to each other from beginning to end. House explains the why, but also couples that to multiple examples of how, and illustrates it all with writing samples from his students. Moreover, he eventually shows how the many activities and readings, with theory acting as glue, coalesce into a cohesive writing program.

That sense of seemingly disparate components coming together to form a dialogical whole informs ***Blending Genre, Altering Style: Writing Multigenre Papers*** (2010) by **Tom Romano.** Inspired in part by Michael Ondaatje's *The Collected Works of Billy the Kid*, Romano evolved the idea of having students write on subjects of interest using a range of genres to piece together a collective argument. Like the other authors discussed in this essay, Romano clearly lays out a theoretical foundation and then enhances the design with a vivid discussion of how best to implement such work in the classroom. In particular, he notes that multigenre efforts have the best chance of success when teachers "provide models of such papers, lead students into prompts that enable them to experiment with various genres and writing strategies, hold conferences with them, and devote class time to the development of their writing within a community of sharing" (p. 4). As someone who has preservice and inservice teachers create a multigenre paper as part of course requirements, I can vouch for his advice, as well as the dialogical atmosphere it sustains.

Finally, if Romano asks students to play with genre, then **Ralph Fletcher** in his ***Pyrotechnics on the Page: Playful Craft That Sparks Writing*** (2010) expects young writers to muck with the language contained within genre. Like Ray's book, it's geared for K–8 learners, but also like her book, the possibilities for high school classrooms are evident and plentiful. Too often, language study and writing have been turned into drudge work, particularly in this age of micromanaged classrooms. Fletcher, admitting his debt to writer and writing teacher Don Murray, seeks to reunite students and teachers with pleasures of noodling with words. He argues, and I agree, that "[w]riters play with language" (p. 2) and that such play goes hand-in-hand with the creation of meaning. Through the book, he shows how he, other authors, and students bring this belief to realization.

For me, the key thread that stitches these book selections together is that they engage the reader in dialogue. Each has a stance and a set of beliefs and each argues well for those perspectives. But each also leaves rooms for teachers to imagine these ideas in their classrooms and to make the necessary shifts that would go with their evolving context. Whether it's Hillocks on narrative, Katie Wood Ray on reading as writers, Maisha Fisher on the power of urban poetry, Jeff House on inductive writing, Tom Romano on multigenre response, or Ralph Fletcher on language play, each invites you to engage in a dialogue of becoming, one that asks you to imagine each classroom through your eyes.

Works Cited

Ensler, E., Sunshine, G., Katz, J., Gavin, M., & Jenkins, C. (Producers), & Sunshine, G., Katz, J., & Gavin, M. (Directors). (2004). *What I want my words to do to you* [DVD]. USA: PBS Home Video.

Fisher, M. T. (2007). *Writing in rhythm: Spoken word poetry in urban classrooms*. New York: Teachers College Press.

Fletcher, R. (2010). *Pyrotechnics on the page: Playful craft that sparks writing*. Portland, ME: Stenhouse.

Goldberg, N. (2005). *Writing down the bones: Freeing the writer within*. Boston: Shambhala.

Hillocks, G. Jr. (2007). *Narrative writing: Learning a new model for teaching*. Portsmouth, NH: Heinemann.

House, J. (2006). *Writing is dialogue: Teaching students to think (and write) like writers*. Norwood, MA: Christopher-Gordon.

Jensen, D. (2004). *Walking on water: Reading, writing, and revolution*. White River Junction, VT: Chelsea Green.

Lamott, A. (1994). *Bird by bird: Some instructions on writing and life*. New York: Pantheon.

O'Connor, F. (1979). *Mystery and manners: Occasional prose*. New York: Farrar, Straus and Giroux.

Ray, K. W. (1999). *Wondrous words: Writers and writing in the elementary classroom*. Urbana, IL: National Council of Teachers of English.

Romano, T. (2000). *Blending genre, altering style: Writing multigenre papers*. Portsmouth, NH: Boynton/Cook.

Ueland, B. (2007). *If you want to write: A book about art, independence, and spirit*. St. Paul, MN: Graywolf Press.

Works Cited

Adler, M., & Rougle, E. (2005). *Building literacy through class-room discussion: Research-based strategies for developing critical readers and thoughtful writers in middle school.* New York: Scholastic.

Albom, M. (1997). *Tuesdays with Morrie: An old man, a young man, and life's greatest lesson.* New York: Doubleday.

Anyon, J. (1997). *Ghetto schooling: A political economy of urban educational reform.* New York: Teachers College Press.

Anzaldúa, G. (2007). *Borderlands/La frontera.* San Francisco: Aunt Lute Books.

Arad, A., Ziskin, L., & Curtis, G. (Producers), & Raimi, S. (Director). (2002–2007). *Spider-Man* [Motion Picture]. USA: Sony Pictures.

Bakhtin, M. M. (1981). Discourse in the novel (C. Emerson & M. Holquist, Trans.). In M. Holquist (Ed.), *The dialogic imagination: Four essays by M. M. Bakhtin.* (pp. 259–422). Austin: University of Texas Press.

Bakhtin, M. M. (1986). *Speech genres and other late essays* (C. Emerson & M. Holquist, Eds.; V. W. McGee, Trans.). Austin: University of Texas Press.

Banks, R. (1995). *Rule of the bone.* New York: Harper Collins.

Berthoff, A. E. (1984). Is teaching still possible? Writing, meaning, and higher order reasoning. *College English, 46*(8), 743–755.

Blasingame, J., & Bushman, J. H. (2005). *Teaching writing in middle and secondary schools.* Upper Saddle River, NJ: Pearson Merrill Prentice Hall.

Bono. (1984). Pride. On *The unforgettable fire* [vinyl]. Santa Monica, CA: Island Records.

Bradbury, R. (1996). *Zen in the art of writing.* Santa Barbara, CA: Joshua Odell Editions.

Bruffee, K. A. (1984). Collaborative learning and the "conversation of mankind." *College English, 46*(7), 635–652.

Cameron, J., & Landau, J. (Producers) & Cameron, J. (Director). (1997). *Titanic* [Motion Picture]. USA: Paramount.

Cisneros, S. (1984). *The house on Mango Street.* New York: Knopf Doubleday Publishing Group.

Coalition of Essential Schools. (2010). *Less is more, depth over coverage.* Retrieved from http://www.essentialschools.org/principles/10.

Cochran-Smith, M., & Lytle, S. L. (1993). *Inside/outside: Teacher research and knowledge.* New York: Teachers College Press.

Coles, G. (2003). *Reading the naked truth: Literacy, legislation, and lies.* Portsmouth, NH: Heinemann.

Collier, B. (2000). *Uptown.* New York: Henry Holt.

Daniels, H., Zemelman, S., & Steineke, N. (2007). *Content-area writing: Every teacher's guide.* Portsmouth, NH: Heinemann.

Darling-Hammond, L. (2004). From "separate but equal" to "no child left behind": The collision of new standards and old inequalities. In D. Meier & G. Wood (Eds.), *Many children left behind: How the No Child Left Behind Act is damaging our children and our schools* (pp. 3–32). Boston: Beacon Press.

Dewey, J. (1938). *Experience and education.* New York: Macmillan.

Dickens, C. (1940). *A tale of two cities.* New York: Grosset and Dunlap.

Elbow, P. (1981). *Writing with power: Techniques for mastering the writing process.* New York: Oxford University Press.

Emig, J. (1971). *The composing processes of twelfth graders.* Urbana, IL: National Council of Teachers of English.

Ensler, E. (1998). *The vagina monologues.* New York: Villard.

Ewald, W. (2002). *The best part of me: Children talk about their bodies in pictures and words.* New York: Little, Brown.

Fecho, B. (2004). *"Is this English?" Race, language, and culture in the classroom.* New York: Teachers College Press.

Fecho, B., Collier, N. D., Friese, E. E. G., & Wilson, A. A. (2010). Critical conversations: Tensions and opportunities of the dialogical classroom. *English Education, 42*(4), 427–447.

Finn, P. J. (1999). *Literacy with an attitude: Educating working-class children in their own self-interest.* Albany: State University of New York Press.

Flower, L. (1981). *Problem-solving strategies for writing.* New York: Harcourt Brace Jovanovich.

Forster, E. M. (1950). *Howards end.* New York: Alfred A. Knopf.

Frank, A. (1993). *Anne Frank: The diary of a young girl.* New York: Bantam.

Freire, P. (1970). *Pedagogy of the oppressed.* New York: Continuum.

Fullan, M. (1993). *Change forces: Probing the depths of educational reform.* New York: Falmer Press.

Giroux, H. A. (1988). *Teachers as intellectuals: Toward a critical pedagogy of learning.* Granby, MA: Bergin and Garvey.

Goodlad, J. I. (1984/2004). *A place called school: Promise for the future.* New York: McGraw-Hill.

Gordimer, N. (1991). Once upon a time. In *Jump and other stories* (pp. 23–30). New York: Farrar, Straus & Giroux.

Gordon, L. R. (2000). *Existentia Africana: Understanding Africana existential thought.* New York: Routledge.

Goswami, D., & Stillman. P. R. (Eds.). (1987). *Reclaiming the classroom: Teacher research as an agency for change.* Upper Montclair, NJ: Boynton/Cook.

Graves, D. H. (1983). *Writing: Teachers and children at work.* Exeter, NH: Heinemann.

Greene, J. P. (2002). High school graduation rates in the United States. Retrieved from http://www.manhattan-institute.org/html/cr_baeo.htm.

Gutiérrez, K. D., Asato, J., Pacheco, M., Moll, L. C., Olson, K., Horng, E. L., Ruiz, R., García, E., & McCarty, T. L. (2002). "Sounding American": The consequences of new reforms on English language learners. *Reading Research Quarterly, 37*(3), 328–343.

Hansen, J., Newkirk, T., & Graves, D. (1985). *Breaking ground: Teachers relate reading and writing in the elementary school.* Portsmouth, NH: Heinemann.

Havelock-Allen, A., Brabourne, J., & Goodwin, R. B. (producers), & Zeffirelli, F. (Director). (2000). *Romeo and Juliet* [DVD]. USA: Paramount.

Heaney, S. (1966). Blackberry picking. In *Death of a naturalist.* New York: Oxford University Press.

Heath, S. B. (1983). *Ways with words: Language, life, and work in communities and classrooms.* Cambridge, UK: Cambridge University Press.

Hemingway, E. (1970). *The fifth column* and four unpublished stories of the Spanish Civil War: *The denunciation, The butterfly and the tank, Night before battle, Under the ridge.* New York: Bantam Books.

Hermans, H. J. M., & Kempen, H. J. G. (1993). *The dialogical self: Meaning as movement.* San Diego: Academic Press.

Hillocks, G., Jr. (2007). *Narrative writing: Learning a new model for teaching.* Portsmouth, NH: Heinemann.

Hooks, K., Sacks, A., & Morgan, C. (Producers), & Hooks, K. (Director). (2000). *The color of friendship* [VHS]. USA/Canada: Alan Sacks Productions.

Hudson, R. (Producer), & Houston, R. (Director). (2004). *Mighty times: The children's march* [DVD]. USA: HBO Family.

Jackson, P., Osborne, B., Walsh, F., Ordesky, M. (Producers), & Jackson, P. (Director). (2001–2003). *The lord of the rings* [Motion Picture]. New Zealand: WingNut Films.

Jensen, D. (2004). *Walking on water: Reading, writing, and revolution.* White River Junction, VT: Chelsea Green Publishing.

Jillette, P. (2009). Commentary: Is Obama skidding or crashing? Retrieved from http://www.cnn.com/2009/POLITICS/04/01/jillette.skid/index.html.

Kamler, B. (2001). *Relocating the personal: A critical writing pedagogy.* Albany: State University of New York Press.

Keneally, T. (1982). *Schindler's list.* New York: Simon and Schuster.

Kohn, A. (2000). *The case against standardized testing: Raising the scores, ruining the schools.* Portsmouth, NH: Heinemann.

Kopkind, A. (1995). *The Thirty Years' Wars: Dispatches and diversions of a radical journalist 1965–1994.* New York: Verso.

Laird, J., DeBell, M., & Chapman, C. (2006). *Dropout rates in the United States: 2004* (NCES Publication No. 2007-024). Retrieved from US Department of Education, National Center for Education Statistics website: http://nces.ed.gov/pubs2007/2007024.pdf

Langer, J. A. (2001). Beating the odds: Teaching middle and high school students to read and write well. *American Educational Research Journal, 38*(4), 837–880.

Lee, H. (1960). *To kill a mockingbird.* New York: Warner Books.

Luhrmann, B., & Martinelli, G. (Producers), & Luhrmann, B. (Director). (1996). *Romeo + Juliet* [Motion Picture]. USA: Twentieth Century Fox.

Lysaker, J. T. (2006). Young children's readings of wordless picture books: What's "self" got to do with it? *Journal of Early Childhood Literacy, 6*(1), 33–55.

MacGillivray, L., Ardell, A. L., Curwen, M. S., & Palma, J. (2004). Colonized teachers: Examining the implementation of a scripted reading program. *Teaching Education, 15*(2), 131–144.

Macrorie, K. (1988). *The I-search paper: Revised edition of searching writing.* Portsmouth, NH: Boynton/Cook.

Marvel, J., Lyter, D. M., Peltola, P., Strizek, G. A., & Morton, B. A. (2007). *Teacher attrition and mobility: Results from the 2004–05 teacher follow-up survey* (NCES Publication No. 2007-307). Retrieved from US Department of Education, National Center for Education Statistics website: http://nces.ed.gov/pubs2007/2007307.pdf.

McCall, N. (1994). *Makes me wanna holler: A young Black man in America.* New York: Random House.

McClintock, M. (2000). How to interrupt oppressive behavior. In M. Adams, W. J. Blumenfield, R. Castañeda, H. W.

Hackman, M. L. Peters, & X. Zúñiga (Eds.), *Readings for diversity and social justice: An anthology on racism, antisemitism, sexism, heterosexism, ableism, and classism* (pp. 483–485). New York: Routledge.

McKenna, M. C., & Robinson, R. D. (2009). *Teaching through text: Reading and writing in the content areas.* Boston: Allyn and Bacon.

Meier, D., & Wood, G. (Eds.). (2004). *Many children left behind: How the No Child Left Behind Act is damaging our children and our schools.* Boston: Beacon Press.

Murray, D. M. (1997). Teach writing as a process not product. In V. Villanueva, Jr. (Ed.), *Cross-talk in comp theory: A reader* (pp. 3–6). Urbana, IL: National Council of Teachers of English.

Nystrand, M. (with Gamoran, A., Kachur, R., and Prendergast, C.). (1996). *Opening dialogue: Understanding the dynamics of language and learning in the English classroom.* New York: Teachers College Press.

Oakes, J. (1985/2005). *Keeping track: How schools structure inequality.* New Haven, CT: Yale University Press.

O'Connor, F. (1979). *Mystery and manners: Occasional prose.* New York: Farrar, Straus and Giroux.

Ondaatje, M. (1970). *The collected works of Billy the Kid: Left-handed poems.* Toronto, Canada: Anansi.

Park, C. L., & Blumberg, C. J. (2002). Disclosing trauma through writing: Testing the meaning-making hypothesis. *Cognitive Therapy and Research, 26*(5), 597–616.

Pipher, M. (2006). *Writing to change the world.* New York: Riverhead Books.

Pratt, M. (1991). Arts of the contact zone. *Profession, 91*, 33–40.

Quantz, R. A., Rogers, J., & Dantley, M. (1991). Rethinking transformative leadership: Toward democratic reform of schools. *Journal of Education, 173*(3), 96–118.

Ravel, M. (1909). *Gaspard de la nuit: Trois poèmes pour piano d'après Aloysius Bertrand* [Recorded by Martha Argerich]. On *Martha Argerich: Live from the Concertgebouw 1978/1979* [CD]. London: EMI Classics. (2001).

Ray, K. W. (1999). *Wondrous words: Writers and writing in the elementary classroom.* Urbana, IL: National Council of Teachers of English.

Romano, T. (1995). *Writing with passion: Life stories, multiple genres.* Portsmouth, NH: Boynton/Cook.

Romano, T. (2000). *Blending genre, altering style: Writing multi-genre papers.* Portsmouth, NH: Boynton/Cook.

Rosenblatt, L. M. (1994). The transactional theory of reading and writing. In R. B. Ruddell, M. R. Ruddell, & H. Singer (Eds.), *Theoretical models and processes of reading* (4th ed., pp. 1057–1092). Newark, DE: International Reading Association.

Rosenblatt, L. M. (1995). *Literature as exploration* (5th ed.). New York: Modern Language Association.

Rylant, C. (1994). *Something permanent.* San Diego: Harcourt Brace.

Santos, A. (2000). Cuando volveras [Recorded by Aventura]. On *Generation Next* [CD]. New York: Premium Latin Music.

Schön, D. A. (1983). *The reflective practitioner: How professionals think in action.* New York: Basic Books.

Schultz, B. D. (2008). *Spectacular things happen along the way: Lessons from an urban classroom.* New York: Teachers College Press.

Shakespeare, W. (1964). *Hamlet.* New York: St. Martin's Press.

Shor, I. (1992). Empowering education: Critical teaching for social change. Chicago: University of Chicago Press.

Sizer, T. R. (1984/2004). *Horace's compromise: The dilemma of the American high school.* Boston: Houghton Mifflin.

Smagorinsky, P. (2002). *Teaching English through principled practice.* Upper Saddle River, NJ: Merrill Prentice Hall.

Smith, F. (2006). *Reading without nonsense* (4th ed.). New York: Teachers College Press.

Sophocles. (1999). *Antigone.* New York: Cambridge University Press.

Soto, G. (1995). Oranges. Retrieved from http://www.english forums.com/English/OrangesByGarySoto/zzrpq/post.htm.

Spiegelman, A. (1983). *Maus I: A survivor's tale: My father bleeds history.* New York: Pantheon Books.

Stigwood, R. (Producer), & Badham, J. (Director). (1977). *Saturday night fever* [Motion Picture]. USA: Paramount.

Stock, P. L. (1995). The dialogic curriculum: Teaching and learning in a multicultural society. Portsmouth, NH: Boynton/Cook.

Swanson, C. B. (2004). *The new math on graduation rates.* Retrieved from http://www.urban.org/url.cfm?ID=1000675.

Tejeda, S. (2006). Shorty, shorty [Recorded by Xtreme]. On *Haciendo Historia* [CD]. Woodland Hills, CA: La Calle Records.

Thalberg, I. (Producer), & Cukor, G. (Director). (1936). *Romeo and Juliet.* USA: Metro-Goldwyn-Mayer.

Ueland, B. (2007). *If you want to write: A book about art, independence and spirit.* St. Paul, MN: Graywolf Press.

Van Wyhe, T. L. C. (2000). A passion for poetry: Breaking rules and boundaries with online relationships. *English Journal, 90*(2), 60–67.

Villanueva, V., Jr. (Ed.). (1997). *Cross-talk in comp theory: A reader.* Urbana, IL: National Council of Teachers of English.

Vygotsky, L. S. (1962). *Thought and language* (E. Hanfmann & G. Vakar, Eds. & Trans.). Cambridge, MA: MIT Press.

Wiesel, E. (1982). *Night.* New York: Bantam Books.

Wiggins, G. (1989). The futility of trying to teach everything of importance. *Educational Leadership, 47*(3), 44–48, 57–59.

Wiggins, G. (1998). *Educative assessment: Designing assessments to inform and improve student performance.* San Francisco: Jossey-Bass.

Wiggins, G., & McTighe, J. (2005). *Understanding by design.* Alexandria, VA: Association for Supervision and Curriculum Development.

Williams, W. C. (1962). This is just to say. Retrieved from http://www.poets.org/viewmedia.php/prmMID/15535.

Woodson, J. (2003). *Locomotion.* New York: G. P. Putnam's Sons.

X, M., & Haley, A. (1965). *The autobiography of Malcolm X.* New York: Grove Press.

Index

Student performance, fears about, 19–22

Talking, relationship with writing, xviii–xix
Teachers, dialogical, qualities of, 35–51
Teaching of writing
    NCTE beliefs about, xi–xxiii, xiii
Texts
    relationship to, 2
    responding to, 6
Thinking, writing as tool for, xiii–xiv, 19–22
Thomas, D., 30
Thoreau, H. D., 46
Turpin, R., 30, 37–38, 85–87, 88
    writing project of, 85–87

Ueland, B., 28, 104
U2, 79

Van Whye, T., 23
Villanueva, V., 18
Vygotsky, L., 37

Who Are You (WAY) project, 86–87
Wiesel, E., 86
Wiggins, G., 22, 58, 64, 87, 96
Wilde, J., 23
Williams, W. C., 84
Wilson, A. A., 45–47, 49, 72–74, 75–77, 87–88
    writing project of, 75–77
Winikur, G., 28
Wood, G., 101

Woodson, J., 69
Workload, fears about, 22–25
Writers, views on writing, 103–6
Writing
    assessment of, xxii–xxiii. *See also* Assessment of writing
    capacity for, xi
    context for, 8–9
    conventions of, xv–xvii
    learning to write by, xi, 28–29
    modalities for, xx–xxi
    office cubicles metaphor of, 91–92
    as process, xii, 17–19
    providing opportunities for, xi–xii
    purposes for, xiv–xv
    relationship with reading, xvii–xviii, 22–25
    relationship with talking, xviii–xix
    social relationships and, xix–xx, 25–28
    teaching of, xi–xxiii
    technology implications for, xx–xxi
    as tool for thinking, xiii–xiv, 19–22
Writing projects, 53–71
    crafting of, 57–69
    extended, 75–83
    framework for, 55–57
    long-term, reflective, 83–87
    mid-range, 63–69
    short-range, 58–63

Zeffirelli, F., 6
Zemelman, S., 21

Author

Bob Fecho is a professor in the Language and Literacy Education Department at the University of Georgia in Athens. To date, his work has focused on issues of language, identity, sociocultural perspectives, practitioner research, and dialogical pedagogy as they relate to adolescent literacy, particularly among marginalized populations. He has published articles in *Harvard Educational Review*, *Journal of Literacy Research*, *Research in the Teaching of English*, and *English Education*, and is the recipient of both the Richard Meade and Alan C. Purves Awards given by the National Council of Teachers of English. One of his books, *"Is This English?" Race, Language, and Culture in the Classroom*, tells of his experiences teaching across cultures in an urban school and was awarded the James N. Britton Award for teacher research from NCTE, along with receiving honorable mention for the 2004 Gustavus Myers Outstanding Book Award given by the Gustavus Myers Center for the Study of Bigotry and Human Rights. Another book, one focused on developing the stance of a dialogical teacher, will be published in 2011. When not visiting his daughters, Cori and Kami, and granddaughter Maeve, he and his partner Janette enjoy traveling, movies, and performing in a folk trio.

This book was typeset in Jansen Text and BotonBQ by
Barbara Frazier.

Typefaces used on the cover include American Typewriter,
Frutiger Bold, Formata Light, and Formata Bold.

The book was printed on 60-lb. Williamsburg
Recycled Offset paper by Versa Press, Inc.